Blackburn
with
Darwen
Memories

Congratulations to the HIVE Award Winners 2017

*Enjoy looking back on how Blackburn became
such a great place to live, work and do business.*

With compliments of **Precision Polymer Engineering Ltd**
See our story on page 112

The publishers would like to thank the following companies for their

support in the production of this book

ACME Refrigeration

Ainsworth Jewellers

Blackburn College

CSH Transport & Forwarding Ltd

Educational Printing Services

Heritage Envelopes

Edwin Ainsworth Ltd

Parkinson Signs

Precision Polymer Engineering

The Mall

Queen Elizabeth's Grammar School

Robinsons Holidays

First published in Great Britain by True North Books Limited
England HX3 6SN
01422 244555
www.truenorthbooks.com
Copyright © True North Books Limited, 2014

Blackburn
with
Darwen
Memories

Contents

Introduction

For all of us, memories are the currency which we use to record the changes and progress in our everyday lives and to fix our place as individuals in the greater scheme of things. This is the latest publication in our 'Memories' series of publications, covering nostalgic reflections of towns and cities throughout the UK. In this new book we will be meandering through a pictorial cross-section of life in Blackburn and Darwen over the last 100 years or so, to help satisfy the longing we all get from time to time, to recall memories of a different era that now seems better or simpler.

As we get older it is often easier to take a step back, and to view events and developments with a clearer sense of prospective. Our aim has been to assist in this respect by presenting a publication relevant to the area capable of rekindling memories of days gone by in an entertaining and informative manner. Looking through the pages of this book it is interesting to reflect on exactly how much change has taken place in the area over a short period, relative to its long history. Many of these photographs are unique and will inevitably remind us of experiences and events in our lives, of our families and of those whose influence and support has touched us to a greater or lesser degree.

Defining features about nostalgia are universal and can bring back fond memories from a time gone by. Recent research shows that nostalgia can counteract loneliness, boredom and anxiety. Couples feel closer and look happier when they're sharing nostalgic memories. People generally get a 'Warm Glow' inside when relating to events and occasions in the past and enjoy reminiscences about how things used to be – even when these events sometimes have a painful side. When people speak wistfully of the past, they typically become more optimistic and inspired about the future.

We can all remember events surrounding friends and family, holidays, weddings, special occasions and nights out in Blackburn and Darwen. So let your mind wander and think of the youthful days at the dance hall or courting in one of the many cinemas in the city. Be entertained as we take you on a sentimental journey through the pages of 'Blackburn with Darwen Memories'…. Happy Memories!

TEXT	BRENDAN O'NEILL, ANDREW MITCHELL, STEVE AINSWORTH
PHOTOGRAPH RESEARCH	BRENDAN O'NEILL
DESIGNER	SEAMUS MOLLOY
BUSINESS DEVELOPMENT MANAGER	PETER PREST

Victorian & Edwardian Blackburn

Left: Long before TV, newsreels, cinema and the rest there was little chance for the general public to see much of the Royal Family. Perhaps it was partly a degree of distance that helped promote feelings of awe in the British, along with loyalty on the part of the Crown's subjects as a matter of course. Whatever the reason, there was a definite essence of national pride that helped unite everyone. That was shown on 9 May, 1888, when the Prince and Princess of Wales, the future King Edward VII and Queen Alexandra, came to town. Here, on Preston New Road, opposite Shear Bank Road, a welcoming arch was created by members of the police fire brigade volunteers. Two-wheeled fire escapes were used as the framework and a pair of fire officers posed there as the photographer captured the scene for posterity.

Below and right: The processions date from either side of the First World War. The later one on Rishton's High Street was taken at a time when women had started to take on board their new roles in society as people with a vocal and political presence. Mrs Pankhurst and her suffragettes had made sure of that. By 1920, partial voting rights were theirs, becoming full participants at the polling booths by the end of the decade. This was only just, especially in the light of the sacrifices made and commitment shown in 1914-18, taking on male roles in transport, industry and agriculture. Note, too, the difference in the attire of those on parade, compared with that shown by their counterparts from 1900. Gone are the decorous, but largely impractical flowing dresses and fine wide-brimmed hats, festooned with feathers and other fripperies. They have been replaced with more functional clothing, though attractive enough on the fashionable eye of the period. The older photograph shows members of Rishton Parish Church demonstrating their Anglican beliefs in harness with their handsome apparel. In the 19th century, religious services in the Great Harwood and Rishton areas were held in a variety of places, including workers' cottages. By the 1860s, the local population had topped 1,000 and the decision was made to build a school church. This was licensed for services in 1866. Just over ten years later, the Church of St Peter and St Paul on Blackburn Road was built and consecrated on 14 June, 1877.

Above: This is not a scene which many would recognise in today's Blackburn Centre as much of it fell foul of the modernisation of the 1960s. It is, in fact, a view of Victoria Street looking across Market Place at the turn of the last century. Today, you would need to walk to the end of Victoria Street before you could see the recognisable dome of St Johns Church, which in this photograph is in the far distance. It was not an easy task for the photographers of the day, as long exposures onto glass plates meant the subjects had to remain stationary for 2 or 3 minutes. The delivery boys in the foreground did just this, however, we can see those in the middle of the square have blurred due to their movement. Tea was a popular drink of the day and a real preference for the Temperance Society of the time and we can see at leats three shops advertising their different brands of tea for sale.

Below: The Bay Horse at 1 Salford, stood at the junction with Church Street and Ainsworth Street. It is yet another of those traditional town centre pubs that is lost forever, only to be recalled in distant memories or with the help of photography. The 1906 picture includes evidence that some of those famous shire horses might have passed by recently. After all, this was a Thwaites' pub and the horse drawn drays were part of that brewery's heritage and a recognisable part of its daily business. The local firm was founded in 1807 by Daniel Thwaites. A year later, he married Betty Duckworth, daughter of the part owner of Eanam Brewery. When she inherited his share, the growth of the Thwaites' empire began. Today, it boasts 350 pubs across the North of England.

Above: Now called the Victoria Building, this was the original Blackburn Technical College on Feilden Street. The idea for such a seat of learning was floated in 1886, but initially garnered little interest. Things changed the following year when the Queen celebrated her golden jubilee and it was decided to mark the occasion with the founding of a school such as this. The Prince and Princess of Wales were invited to lay the foundation stone on 9 May, 1888. The first students were admitted in September the following year to a building that had rooms on four levels, with outdoor sheds for those studying textiles. Other buildings have been added since the 1960s and the campus now offers part and full time courses for about 15,000 students.

Bottom left and below: These views are from times about a quarter of a century apart. The one with the cars on show will have been captured in the 1920s, but the earlier scene contains similar activity taking place. The first town markets would have been held in the Cathedral grounds, but by 1101 formal permission had been granted to hold one in an area enclosed by Church Street, Darwen Street, Mill Lane, Market Street Lane and Astley Gate. After centuries of change and development, the distinctive Market House, as it was known, opened in 1848. A 72 feet high tower or campanile was its companion and in 1877 a decision was taken to add a time ball. The architectural crime of bulldozing the market buildings to make way for new ones took place in the 1960s.

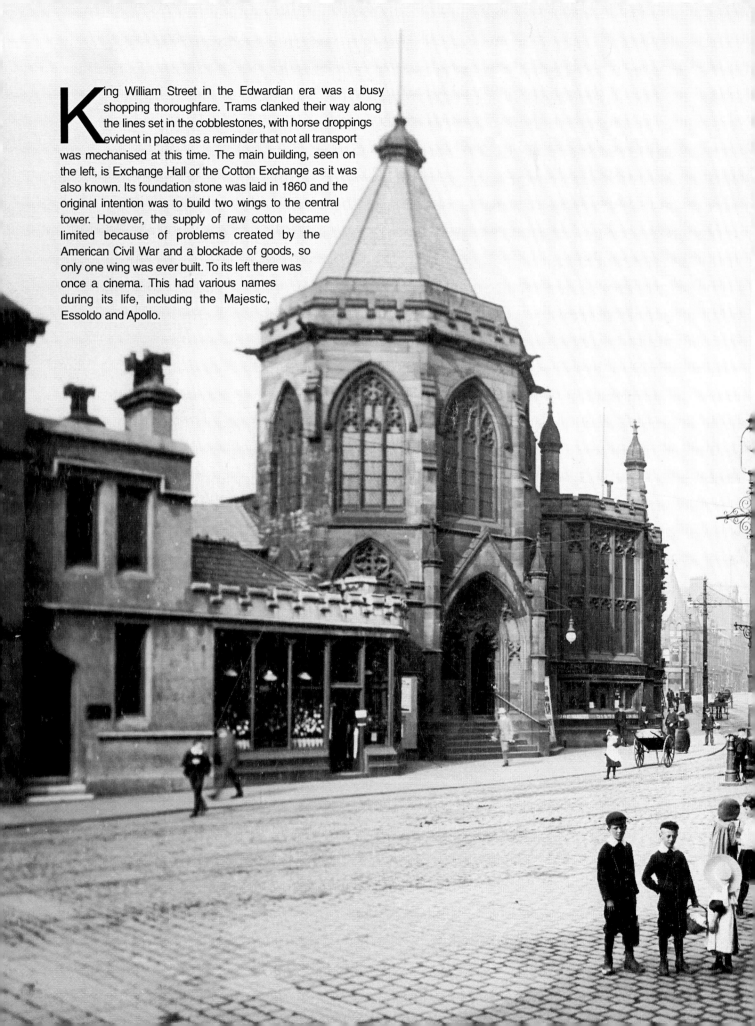

King William Street in the Edwardian era was a busy shopping thoroughfare. Trams clanked their way along the lines set in the cobblestones, with horse droppings evident in places as a reminder that not all transport was mechanised at this time. The main building, seen on the left, is Exchange Hall or the Cotton Exchange as it was also known. Its foundation stone was laid in 1860 and the original intention was to build two wings to the central tower. However, the supply of raw cotton became limited because of problems created by the American Civil War and a blockade of goods, so only one wing was ever built. To its left there was once a cinema. This had various names during its life, including the Majestic, Essoldo and Apollo.

No wonder men and little lads gathered to gawp. The woman doing her shopping at the fruit and veg market stall was very racy looking, considering this was 1906. Edwardian England was not really ready for a very early Mary Quant. An older woman nearby has a decidedly grim and disapproving look on her face. The corresponding image of market life shows women more conventionally attired. That picture was taken some time later, in 1912, and women in skirt hems just above the norm were much more typical of the fashion of the day. It was only after the Great War and the coming of the flapper age in the Roaring Twenties that it was generally seen as acceptable to have more leg on display.

Through The Town

Above and right: It was Easter 1927 when a fleet of charabancs queued on Blackburn Boulevard in readiness to whisk off day trippers to the seaside. The Golden Mile at Blackpool lay ready and waiting for all those fun seekers keen to get a break from their daily toil in the cotton mills. It looks to have been a bright and sunny day, so they should have been in luck. This was just as well, as a number of the vehicles were open topped, converted lorries. The Leyland Lion in the middle of the photo saw service on the Mill Hill route at that time. The 1925 companion image shows Station Square.

Top right: .The Salford area of Blackburn was a bustling thriving part of the town around 1910 with the scene showing the tram lines running through the stone setts in the road. The fine Victorian buildings in the centre of the shot show Thomas Cooks Tourist Excursions and Shipping Office and the Great Northern Railway Offices. Between these two prominent businesses sits J Boyle and Co's confectioners advertising their 'Jap Nuggets', a sweet made from white sugar, semolina and coconut. These could well have been James Boyles' or 'Toffy Jem' as he was know, best seller of the day.

Above: A very quiet day in Darwen around 1910 with only one car visible on Bolton Road and a few pedestrians ambling up the pavement on the opposite side. Surprisingly, it is not a much changed scene today, in terms of the buildings shown here, although the tram lines have long disappeared and the traffic has increased significantly. The George pub remains as a building, on the right just where the pedestrians are, however, its future as a pub, at the time of writing, is uncertain. The large building at the junction is now the NatWest bank. The lone car is parked outside a fine building which is now an opticians and it is unlikely the driver would have been seeking an eye test in this era. A very striking conical roof in the distance also remains and can be found above the redbrick building at the corner of Croft Street today, which at present is being sold by auction. So its is pleasing to note that Darwens' central buildings have stood the tests of time and no doubt many memories will be triggered by this photo.

Right: The Town Hall cost about £35,000 to build, which is equivalent to about £1.5 million in today's currency. It was designed by James Patterson and built by Hacking and Stones. As well as having a large assembly room and council chamber, it was here that the Central Police Station and its 18 cells were based. Nowadays, the headquarters of the Eastern Division of the Lancashire Constabulary can be found on the edge of town at Whitebirk Drive. It was much easier to make direct contact in 1932. It also seemed that you were more likely to see a bobby patrolling the streets than happens in modern times. To some, that is progress, but to others it is just another example of what Max Bygraves described in his song, 'Fings Ain't Wot They Used T'Be'.

Above: The building in the centre of this photo of Darwen Circus in the late 1940s, is the Millstone Hotel, which remains with the Thwaites Brewery today. The hotel has been a popular watering hole for locals for many years and given its position in the centre of Darwen it is hoped this will continue for many years to come. The street where the Austin is emerging from has now been pedestrianised, but the terraced shops opposite the Millstone continue with a newsagents, Printer Cartridge shop and Estate Agents. Unfortunately, the ornate, black and white Jacobean building to the right has lost its upper floor and has become the single story HSBC bank. All in all not a huge change to the centre, but one which has meant the scene seems a little less picturesque and possibly more frenetic today.

Left: Those first years after the last war were difficult times for us all. We were in debt to the Americans for billions and we would never again regain the important standing we had as a world power. Some said that we had won the war but had to surrender the peace. Rationing still bit hard in the late 1940s, so some of the goods on display along King William Street needed us to save up coupons as well as cash if we wanted to do anything more than a little bit of window shopping. Much of the area was remodelled in the 1960s and 70s and most of the retail outlets are now situated in pedestrianised parts.

Above: The Vee Cross Café was a good place to get a morning cuppa while you took a break from the chores of doing the week's shopping in the town centre. Situated on the corner of Charlotte Street and Victoria Street, it was a handy meeting place for housewives to have a natter before carrying on with what was still regarded as the woman's job. The carpet shop downstairs was offering a few sale bargains, but in 1955 money was still a bit tight. Postwar austerity was not as bad as it had been, but no-one had money to burn in 1955. But things would pick up and, in a few years' time, Prime Minister Macmillan would tell us all that we had 'never had it so good'.

Bottom left: The Golden Lion stood at 51 Church Street. The pub was connected to the Golden Lion Vaults on the corner of Ainsworth Street with Victoria Street. In its heyday, the pub had a fine reputation as a coaching inn. There was a spacious rear courtyard and accompanying stables. Stagecoaches went from here to Liverpool and various other parts of the northwest and beyond. Seen here in 1952, it was part of a local brewery's empire. Thomas Dutton and son, William, established a business at Salford on land rented from the Vicar of Blackburn. The brewery was passed down through the generations as a family affair. It grew markedly in the 1920s, buying out a number of smaller enterprises. The company was taken over by Whitbread in 1978 and the brewery demolished in 1986. Morrison's supermarket stands there now. The Golden Lion was knocked down to make way for the Arndale Centre development.

Below: Woolworth's was, for most of the last century, a familiar name on every high street in the land. Seen here in 1958, by the roundabout at Salford, this was the original five and ten cent store. Founded in the USA in 1878, the company came to Britain in 1909 when a store was opened in Liverpool. During the interwar years, 'Woolies', as it was affectionately known, boomed. Cheap and cheerful, it attracted so much custom that it seemed it would last forever. Success continued well into the second half of the last century, but by the 1990s the firm's lack of adaptability spelled out its eventual downfall. It could not exist on pick 'n' mix forever. All its stores in the UK closed in late 2008 and early 2009. The Daily Dispatch name on the building to the left of the former Woolworth store refers to the newspaper founded by Edward Hutton in 1900. It had merged with the News Chronicle in 1955 and was later absorbed into the Daily Mail.

Right: It is not just cinemas and pubs that are regarded as having served their purpose and are then condemned to suffer the fate of the wrecking ball. It happens to places of worship as well. In 1965, it was the turn of the Congregational Church at New Wellington Street, Mill Hill, to suffer such a fate. Quite what was so attractive about seeing a religious building brought to the ground is hard to appreciate, but the demolition process had attracted a small crowd of onlookers. The church had held its first service over 100 years earlier, with the inaugural ceremony taking place on 19 September, 1860. The building costs were estimated to be in the region of £6,000. It is thought that, when full, it could accommodate nearly 1,000 worshippers. The last service was held in 1962.

Below: Some readers might remember as children riding on a milk float on a Saturday morning, earning a couple of bob helping with deliveries. If no-one was watching, then we could sometimes persuade the milkman to let us take the wheel for a short distance, but that would have had to have taken place on a quiet street. Normally busy Blakey Moor was not the place to chance being apprehended by the long arm of the law. It was a pleasant summer's day in 1965 as the vehicle that inspired Benny Hill's wonderful song about Ernie's pitched battle with Two Ton Ted is parked to make a delivery. Benny had actually been a milkman in Eastleigh, Hampshire, so knew a lot about gold tops rattling in crates. The handsome building behind the trees is the old Technical College, now part of the University.

Above: This image gives a feel of the upheaval felt in Blackburn in the 1960s due to the redevelopment of the town. Significant demolition had to take place to enable the building of the new Town Hall development. Sadly, for many Blackburn people, this demolition included the old market and its famous clock tower. The Town Hall stands proudly in the background and would remain an iconic building in Blackburn through the redevelopment.

Left and below: The development of Blackburn was progressing at pace in the late 1960s and early 70s. In one photograph we have the controversial high rise construction of the Town Hall extension in 1968. The Anglia, Ford Consul, Austin and Hillman cars parked here confirm the date. In a higher level view we see the changing face of the the middle of Blackburn, with the Central Area Development in 1971. It would take two years to complete the transformation of the Victoria and Ainsworth Street areas.

Entertainment, Leisure & Pastimes

Below: The Bowmen of Pendle and Samlesbury is a long established archery club, open to all ages and both sexes. This fine body of men and women, pictured in 1920, carried on the tradition of our longbowmen in the Hundred Years' War battles of Crécy, Poitiers, Agincourt and the rest. The targets in modern times are circular, rather than Gallic! Originally the Pendle Archers, the club was founded in 1902. Shooting took place in individual members' grounds until a base was found at Clitheroe Polo Club. A new club, the Samlesbury Bowmen, was formed in 1930. The rivals amalgamated under the present joint name two years later, using Samlesbury Hall as its home. In 2006, it moved to a new home at Nab's Head Lane.

Below right: The boathouse on the lake in Queen's Park, viewed here in 1920, remains a major feature of this leisure facility, just as it has been for over a century since the Victorian structure was built. At the height of its popularity, boats could be seen scudding across the water as visitors enjoyed themselves in harmless fun. Sadly, the hiring of craft to the general public ceased over 30 years ago. The boathouse is used by the youth services and a grand amenity has been lost to locals for more than a generation. The 3.5 acre serpentine lake is laid out in two sections, connected by a narrow channel. The lake is fed by Audley Brook.

Left: The music played in Corporation Park's Bandstand attracted crowds from far and wide. It was a popular event from as far back as 1857 when the first bandstand was built. This photograph shows the newer construction which was erected in September 1909 and had a capacity in the surrounding seats and terraces for around 2,000 people. This event probably took place around the early 1930s and it looks like those standing well outnumbered those in the seats, more than likely this was due to the cost of sitting and listening rather than standing on the outer edges. But everyone will have enjoyed this brass band as a treat on a Sunday afternoon.

Above: The 1935 matinee prices at the Savoy were just 4d (1.7p) or 6d (2.5p), dependent upon whether you wanted a ground floor or balcony seat. Prices doubled for evening performances of 'Forgotten Men'. This was an unusual offering as it was not the normal movie froth, but a documentary aimed at the youth of the day as a warning against the horrors of war. It included interviews with World War One veterans and stark images from that conflict. The picture house was decorated with garlands and bunting to mark the 25th anniversary of King George V's accession to the throne. The building at 36 Bolton Road is still with us, fulfilling a role as a carpet shop of late. The name 'Savoy' is still in use here.

Above: An unusual scene is depicted here and one which was a welcome event at many factories and offices around the country. This photograph shows employees at a Blackburn factory canteen enjoying one of the nation's most popular radio shows of the time, 'Workers Playtime'. Transmitted by the BBC between 1941 and 1964, it was originally intended to boost workers' morale during the war years and toured the country inviting talented workers to join in the show. Guests appearing included Peter Sellers, Morecambe and Wise, Frankie Howard, Ken Dodd and many others. The BBC had only planned for this show to run for six weeks but in fact it became one of the longest running radio shows in history. Not bad for a touring radio show!

Right: The Corporation Baths on Belper Street opened in 1906. As well as the swimming pool there was a 'slipper bath', used by those who did not have the facilities at home to have a proper all over soak. Some families did not even own a zinc bath that could be hung up on a nail and brought into the front room as needed! By the time that these lads were taking the plunge, perhaps inspired by the exploits of Olympic swimmer and movie star Buster Crabbe in the 1930s, the pool had completed over three decades of service to the community. The building, both inside and out, has been remodelled several times in the interim and rebranded as Daisyfield Pools.

became adults in peacetime. Now, they had a new Elizabethan age upon them and hope sprang eternal. Queen's Park opened in 1887 in honour of Victoria's golden jubilee. It is situated about a mile from the town centre, out towards Oswaldtwistle. A pair of trees was planted in front of the boathouse to mark the park's centenary and, five years later in 1992, 40 more were put in place to mark the number of years our present monarch had then served. The other photographs are of Corporation Park. The entrance gates from Preston New Road are seen from just inside the park as they looked in 1935. The lands were opened to the general public on 22 October, 1857. The formal Garden of Remembrance was laid out in 1922 to accompany the War Memorial.

I f ever you feel stressed or need somewhere to blow away those urban blues, just come along to one of the many parks you can find dotted across the area. The serenity of the surroundings will calm you down no end. How can anyone be other than relaxed when taking in the scenery and surroundings that are free for anyone to enjoy? The view across the lake in Queen's Park comes from 1955. The mums pushing their prams around the perimeter of the water hoped for better things for their offspring. As youngsters themselves, they had been born at the start of the Depression in the 1930s, gone to school during the war and endured the continuation of rationing as they

partners with their bopping and jiving skills. The building was converted from the former Olympic Cinema in St Peters Street, by Mecca Ltd and cost £130,000 in 1959. The Locarno attracted an number of top bands at the time and The Who played there in 1966.

Below The idea behind the building of St George's Hall was formulated in the early 1900s when it was decided that those belonging to the council were too small to host large scale entertainment. The foundation stone was laid in 1913, but the Hall was used as a hospital during the 1914-18 War and was not used for its original purpose until 1921. Situated on Blakey Moor, King George's has welcomed the best in the land to tread its boards. Slade appeared on more than one occasion in the 1970s. This midlands glam rock outfit sold more singles in the UK during that decade than any other group. Slade topped the charts on six occasions, with gravel voiced Noddy Holder's 'Merry Christmas Everybody' being the last and most enduring of these.

Above: Hair styles, slick suits and flouncy dresses are a dead giveaway to the era of this photograph, it was, of course, the 'Swinging Sixties'. The venue was Blackburn's Locarno Ballroom, a popular place for the teenagers of the day to show off their new 'trendy gear' and impress their

When Royalty Calls

It was 10th July, 1913, when royalty came to Blackburn in the form of King George V and Queen Mary. They were on a week-long tour of 30 Lancashire towns. The town was transformed for the visit as the council had run competitions for the best decorated premises. Bunting, ribbons and floral decorations adorned the route and industrial premises and offices took on an altogether different look, particularly the gas works. We see here the King and Queen on a stage surrounded by dignitaries. It was the first time a reigning monarch had visited Blackburn and the town was not going to let this go by without the royals feeling that Blackburn was a special and very friendly place. In the close-up of the Queen she is being introduced to Mr John Duckworth by Lord Derby. It is surprising how much taller the queen looks in this photo compared to those around her. She had been crowned two years earlier in Westminster Abbey together with her husband the king.

The crowds turned out again in 1936 for the visit of the Duke of Kent on his tour of East Lancashire. The royal cars line up behind him as he walks from the men's Social Service building. We get a real feel for the pride of the people of Blackburn as they stand smiling and respectful along the street and with just a couple of bobbies in sight, as no one expected any trouble. The sea of flat caps is typical of the time and every vantage point was taken in order to get a better view. In the close-up version we can see the prince chatting with locals along the route outside Carr's Mills. The little girl eager to get a better view and hear what the prince was saying is held firmly by the arm by her mother.

It was the turn of the Royal Ordnance factory in Blackburn in 1941 to receive a royal visit. Below shows King George VI and Queen Elizabeth visiting the factory with local VIPs in recognition of the tremendous work which had been carried out by the factory in support of the war effort. The factory had been deemed so important that it had been painted brown and green to camouflage it and protect it from enemy bombers. A decoy factory had also been built on the nearby moors, to further thwart any possible air raids. The Queen Mother returned to Blackburn in June 1948, (right) and is seen shaking hands with Mrs Annie Wearden at Haston Lee Mill.

The royal visit of 1955 saw the new Queen Elizabeth visit Blackburn on a beautiful summer day. This scene was taken with the Mullard Plant Director Mr C De Wit which the queen had just visited and she stands waving at the crowds of workers who had gathered to cheer her on to her next visit. Mullards Electronic Valves had been developed for the burgeoning electronics industry and would soon be in even greater demand due to the growing popularity of televisions. The two constables to her right still wear their war medals on their uniforms and its is hard to believe that it was only 10 years previously that the terrible conflict had ended. The Queen and the Duke of Edinburgh had been welcomed at Blackburn Town Hall earlier by a Guard of Honour from the 4th Battalion, the East Lancashire Regiment.

A Bit of Shopping

Below: Looking down Church Street in 1930 allows us to see this part of town as our grandparents knew it. Note how nearly everyone seemed to wear some sort of headgear. Women, especially if they wanted to be ladylike, had to wear something smart or be thought to be not properly dressed. The motorbike and sidecar part way down the road was something of a period piece, quite popular in the decades just before and after the last war. It was passing the offices of the merchant Robert Spencer and Sons, formerly of Haigh Coal Yard. This was part of the Wigan Coal and Iron Company that had been formed when the collieries on the Wigan Coalfield owned by John Lancaster were acquired by Lord Lindsay in 1865. At its production peak in the 1920s, this colliery employed over 9,000 workers.

Above: The fruit and vegetable market in Blackburn was a vibrant place in the early hours as produce was delivered and packed ready to be collected by the many green grocery shops from the surrounding areas. These stalls were situated just outside the main Market Hall and maybe a few local shoppers were allowed to buy directly from the wholesalers at a reduced price when the main stock had been sold. It will have certainly been one of the ways that mothers could stretch out their meager housekeeping money in the relatively austere times of the late 1950s.

offee shops were a very new concept when this photograph was taken in November 1952, but we can see that Palatine Dairies Ltd were at the forefront with their coffee and milk bar in Blackburn's old market hall. These bars became ever more popular with the young as a meeting place. Many were built on the American concept but the Italian type Expresso Bar was also popular and could be associated with the Italian film stars of the time such

as Gina Lollobrigida. Palatines, however, would have welcomed the more regular Blackburn shopper and provided a little respite for weary feet and tired legs. Two further views of the inside of the old market hall help to bring back memories of what it was like to shop in the days before supermarkets. Readmans, renowned for its cooked meats and pies, sells bacon at just 7p per pound at today's prices and the stall opposite, Tom Younger Ltd, would be able to clothe for you for any season of the year. The higher level view gives a better feel of the layout of Blackburn's Market Hall.

Shopping in Blackburn Market in the early 1960s was carried out under the watchful eye of the famous clock tower that was so cruelly lost to us all, along with the market hall, over half a century ago. We used to have over 300 stalls, with more than half of these situated on Victoria Street. The tower was unusual in that it held a brass ball that was raised at 12 noon and was lowered again an hour later as a gun was fired. This was an idea used in Greenwich in the mid 19th century as an aid for mariners in helping them set their chronometers accurately. Blackburn was one of the few inland towns to boast such a device. Reid Brothers of London was commissioned to provide the ball and work began in March 1878, taking just two weeks to complete.

Britain. They did not want to dress like their parents or listen to the sort of music that attracted 'the squares' of the older generation. It was out with the old and up with the hemlines. Dickie Valentine was dumped in favour of Billy Fury and life began to move at a much more rapid pace. Even long established firms like Burton's, the 'tailor of taste', felt the pinch. Collarless Beatle jackets, denim jeans and, later on, flower pattern shirts modelled on London's Carnaby Street styles were to become all the rage. No wonder that the Kinks came to sing successfully about a 'Dedicated Follower of Fashion'. Young women looked to models like Jean Shrimpton for their lead. Skirts got shorter and boots higher. Soon, the dresses worn by those women in the 1960 photograph

This trio of shopping scenes, around King William Street and the Church Street junction, comes from the end of the 1950s and early 1960s. This was the time when a shopping revolution began to take shape. The leaders were young people with money in their pockets and, having grown up as postwar baby boomers, they were determined to make their own mark on the High Streets of near the shoe shops of True-Form and Timpson would look very dated. Change was everywhere and this was felt in Downing Street. The old men of the Tory Party found it difficult to attract votes from young people. The likes of Macmillan, Butler and Douglas-Home were seen as fuddy-duddies. Something different was asked for and a Labour government was voted into power for the first time in over a decade.

Right: They may look like a couple of wartime detectives, but in fact these two chaps were from the Weights and Measures Inspectorate. Their job was to make sure that what the public were buying was properly measured out and weighed correctly. You can see the scales being tested at E H Booths in Blackburn in the 1950s. It may look slightly comical but it had a serious purpose and the control of goods being sold can be traced back to the 11th century, when such statements as 'We ordain and command that they shall keep throughout the realm most faithful and marked measures and most faithful and marked weights, as our worthy predecessors have decreed' were made to initiate some from of control over the sale of goods. The jars of Marmite, Lions Treacle and Robinson's Jam seen on these shelves will have been pre-weighed and out of the reach of these two.

Below: The Morris Minors on Astley Gate at the start of the swinging 60s are icons in the history of British motoring. This model made its debut at the Earls Court Motor Show in the early autumn of 1948. Initially available as a two door saloon or convertible tourer, the four door economy family car we grew to love was introduced in 1950. Under the guidance of its creator, Alec Issigonis, over a million left the production lines between then and 1971. The splendid wood framed estate, the Traveller, was first seen in 1952. Issigonis went on to design another famous British car, the Mini, which appeared on our roads at the end of the 1950s.

Right: Self-service supermarkets were still something of a novelty to housewives brought up on corner shops and getting their 'divvi' across the Co-op counter. But to younger women this method of stocking up the household larder was the way forward. The goods priced at the start of the 1970s in old shillings and pence would soon have to have their labelling altered. The marmalade at 1s 6d would become 7.5p and the baked beans re-marked at 5.5p instead of 1s 1d. Decimalisation of our currency took place on 15 February, 1971. The tanner, bob, florin and half crown became obsolete. Traditionalists bemoaned the passing of the old and the arrival of the new, but it did not take long before everyone got used to the replacement coins and terminology.

It wasn't just the markets which attracted the shoppers, Tommy Ball's shoes store was well known throughout the area and Tommy himself was one of life's characters. He had started back in the 1940s as a rag and bone man, pushing a pram and selling second hand clothes and shoes to anyone who would buy them. After he was rejected for a stall on Blackburn Market, he was determined to make a go of it in the shoe trade and built his empire selling shoes across Blackburn, the UK and into Europe. Visitors from across the country would come to Blackburn to buy a pair of Tommy's shoes. Always keen to help the community, his Sunday Shoe Club raised thousands for charity and his Blackburn Exhibition Centre gave new start-ups the chance he never had. Here we have one photo of Tommy's 'Reconditioned Department and one of his

'walkaround store'. Tommy is also pictured with a cheque for charity from his Sunday Club (which required a 5p membership to get around the Sunday Trading Laws). Tommy was a real Blackburn entrepreneur but had to retire in 1986 due to ill health and sadly died at the age of 83 at his home in the Isle of Man.

When We Were Young

Top left: This 1895 photograph shows a classroom of 29 pupils, with the children sat in long bench desks, with curtains at the back and a piano, overseen by two teachers. Education law at the time required that full-time education ceased at the age of eleven when most children would find work in the mills and attend school on a part-time basis only.

Left: It was many years ago at Roe Lee School in 1929 when these infants were photographed, but it hadn't changed much by the 60s and 70s. Occupied by building bricks, crayons and a small rocking horse, these children could play and learn safely in what was a modern new school in Blackburn. The forward thinking planners had provided full height glass doors and a covered veranda which provided a light and airy feel to the classroom. The older children also benefited from this new approach and can be seen sat at their desks in July of the same year, with books open at the ready and all doors open to allow for more air to flow on what looks like a hot summers day.

Above: A little further along the decades we can see children at the old library in Blackburn selecting their favourite books. It's a very typical scene of the time but if you look a bit closer you will see that beneath the school caps and berets, leather satchels were hung around the shoulders, some woollen socks were around the ankles and boots for the boys would stand up to most playground activities. It was 1946 and reading was a popular pastime for children before the invasion of the TV into homes in the mid 1950s.

Above: These four look a happy bunch, with smiles all around. And why not? They had their new uniforms on and were ready to start school at St Stephens in Blackburn in 1954. It was kilts or pleated skirts for the girls and, of course, short pants for the boys, whose shoes are surprisingly the best polished of the four. We have to excuse the little girl at the front as many of you may remember those suede zip boots that were popular at the time, were not to be polished. Blazers and skirts would be handed down to the next child in the family as they were expensive items for mums and dads of the time. Younger family members may

not have liked this but that was the way it was. There were no shopping trips for them at the start of 'big school', although mum or dad would find some other way to make the day special.

Left: Exercise and fresh air were always an enjoyable part of the school day and at Westholme School in the 1950s sports days and gymnastics outside were always popular with the pupils. This display was clearly the boys' prime event to see who could carry who and stay rigid enough so that the whole thing didn't collapse in on itself. It was a hard enough task without having to smile for the camera and some lads on the lower deck looked the other way. There was a similar playground game at the time which was known as 'packhorses' where five or six lads from one team would bend in the same way as the picture. It was then up to their team mates to run and jump, getting as far along the lads' backs, without shuffling along, as they could. The winning team was the one who could get the most boys on the backs of those

creating the 'horse' without it crumbling to the ground. It was always great fun if a little fraught with injuries.

Above: A party in the street would always be a special day for children, but is was not just the day that mattered, it was the build-up and help needed from everyone which was also enjoyable. This event had been organised by the mums and dads of Montague Street, in Blackburn, to celebrate the coronation of Queen Elizabeth in June, 1953. The whole street would take part and although rationing from the war still affected many products, when people pulled together they could always muster up sandwiches, soft drinks and biscuits. In this photo some of the children are tucking into something with their spoons and maybe some enterprising mum or dad had been able to get their hands on jelly and ice cream. Whatever was on the table that day it would only add to the great feeling of a new queen on the throne and certainly helped to bring smiles to the many faces in this shot.

Below: Another event in celebration of the new queen was this puppet show at the Harrison Institute in 1953. These children are enthralled at the dancing figures on stage and would no doubt have understood the importance of the coronation through these clever puppets in a play which was entitled, 'The Coronation Play'. Just look at the faces of the children, open mouthed, with eyes glued to the puppets. It was, of course, before the real introduction of television into the home which would begin around the mid 1950s.

Right: Sunnyhurst Woods in Darwen, was opened in 1903 as a commemoration of Edward VIIs coronation. It was very much down to the Corporation's Parks and Recreation Grounds Committees efforts which created an area where local people could walk, relax and enjoy the beauty of the surrounding woodlands. The corporation built a coupe of ornamental bridges, installed a fountain and created artificial waterfalls above the shallow lake. Here we see mothers with their babies and prams, sitting by the lake on the benches enjoying the sunshine in the late 1940s. It is a wonderful, tranquil scene that can still be enjoyed today.

Below: It wasn't long after the coronation that the children of Blackburn would be able to see royalty in real life on the streets of their town. This was Victoria Street in 1955 with crowds from across Blackburn out to wave flags and cheer for the new Queen Elizabeth. Most of these children were dressed in their school uniforms and all were trying to stay on the pavement to make sure they would not be the ones to hold up the royal cavalcade as it passed.

It almost didn't matter to some children if the paddling pool was full of water or not. In one photo we see children enjoying a splash on what looks like a lovely summer's day at the paddling pool in Queen's Park around the late 1950s. Swimming trunks were not needed if you could roll up your short pants or summer dress and make sure the pants were not going to slip down by making sure your elasticated snake belt was tight enough. The little chap to the right of the railings is waiting to launch his home made boat when things quieten down a little. In Corporation Park some years later we see the paddling pool without water but a little boy enjoying a safe tricycle ride and a little girl playing ball. Mums could sit and chat on the edge of the pool in their floral frocks, without getting their feet wet and it's good to see the swings, roundabout, rocking horse and slide all being put to good use. Back to Queen's Park in 1965, the steps of the slide look a little overcrowded but not as much as the 'bench swing' does, we count around 15 children sat on the swing with one girl at either end pushing them. It was definitely before the days of Health and Safety when compressed rubber bases would replace the concrete and grass and a park warden would ensure only a certain number of children at one time were allowed on each piece of equipment. You have to consider who was having the most fun, the ones in these pictures or those today in the 'controlled parks' we now have in our towns and cities.

On Big Occasions

Below: From the clothing of the onlooking crowd, it would seem that this procession took place in the very early 1900s. It was a notable occasion in the Catholic calendar, so the ladies observing the event put on their best dresses, finest hats and handsome stoles. The men of standing sported natty boaters and homburgs, while the ordinary working men put on their cleanest of flat caps. With the old gas standards as a backdrop, the children made their way along cobbled Rishton Street. Other parishioners followed on behind. This may have been part of the annual Whit Walk when best clothes were always to the fore. However, the white dresses and veils worn by the young girls might alternatively suggest that this was part of the celebrations when kiddies took their first Holy Communion – a real high point in their young lives.

Right: Well, they don't come much bigger than Fred Kempster who toured the country, as part of Astley and Co.'s American Circus. At a height of 7 feet 9 inches, although billed by the circus as 8 feet 4 inches, he was known as the Blackburn Giant or the English Giant. He was born in London in 1889 and after his father's death when he was eight years old, both he and his brother were transferred to a Barnados Home at their mothers request following her struggle to bring up the whole family. Barnados felt that Canada could offer young children the opportunity as farm labourers or domestic and therefore Fred was sent to Canada by the charity. He worked for a family in Manitoba, but his health began to deteriorate after several years. At the age of 15 Fred returned to England, a congenital problem in his knees and tibia had lead to his poor health and his

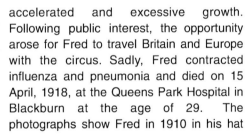

and again a little later showing off his height by shaking hands with a lady in an upstairs window. Fred was buried in a 9-feett coffin in Blackburn Cemetery with his headstone proclaiming him as 'The British Giant'.

Below: It was the impact of India's boycott and increased tariffs on the British cotton industry which prompted the people of Lancashire to ask Mahatma Ghandi to visit Darwen whilst on his visit to England for important governmental talks in 1931. Although he was struck by some of the poverty he saw - almost 10,000 workers had become unemployed because of the actions - he suggested this was little in comparison to the poverty of his own country. The Indian boycott had, in fact, begun because of the mass production of cotton fabrics in Lancashire which had directly impacted the traditional hand loom practices in Indian villages and towns. The visit of Ghandi had been expected to rouse hostilities and the police took precautions to protect this iconic figure. In fact, as Ghandi travelled the town speaking to cotton workers and their families, he received a warm welcome by almost everyone. It was said his warmth and sincerity shone through, although his politics were for his own people.

accelerated and excessive growth. Following public interest, the opportunity arose for Fred to travel Britain and Europe with the circus. Sadly, Fred contracted influenza and pneumonia and died on 15 April, 1918, at the Queens Park Hospital in Blackburn at the age of 29. The photographs show Fred in 1910 in his hat

Above: The young 35-year-old Barbara Castle is on the campaign trail across Blackburn, touring the area and drumming up local support for the upcoming general election. Her vehicle had banners along each side and no doubt a large tannoy system attached precariously to the roof. Such an attractive smile and sincere policies would be sure to win votes which they did, she was elected to parliament succeeding George Ellitson on 27 July, 1945.

Left: Barbara Castle is seen here in 1945 in Blackburn, making a rousing speech in support of her campaign for the much contested Labour seat. She was in fact born in Chesterfield in 1910 and educated at Pontefract High, Bradford Grammar and Oxford University, where she developed her oratory skills and political ambitions.

Left: Well you wouldn't have expected to see a member of parliament taking this pose with a rifle, certainly not with today's media consciousness and political correctness. This is Barbara Castle with 'all guns blazing' at Shorrock Security Ltd, on one of her popular visits. It was one of those opportunities not to be missed for the following photographers, standing MP dressed in an Annie Oakley fashion, it would have no doubt put fear into some of her opponents, albeit in a humorous way.

Below: Her civic duties continued for over 30 years, from 1945 to 1979, as a Labour MP, before being elected to the European Parliament for a further 10 years. She was always willing to support the local community in whatever way she could and her attendance at the opening of the Blackburn Library would have given the event that much more meaning and of course would have been a real delight for the local people and dignitaries attending. She is seen here with the Mayor and Mayoress of Blackburn in 1975. She became Baroness Castle of Blackburn in 1990 and continued in politics right up to her death in May 2002 and was, at that time, the longest serving female MP ever in the House of Commons.

This page: The above photo looks out onto the buses queuing for passengers at Blackburn Station. It's hard to ignore the huge banner or its message above the station entrance. It was, of course, Blackburn's Centenary Year. The town was incorporated in 1851 and a series of celebratory events had been planned to mark the occasion,

including; a procession through the streets, exhibitions, carnivals and dances. The station was the ideal place to let Blackburnians know about the events and visitors to make sure they came back for them. The two chaps with the bicycles may have well been planning what they and their families would be attending. Another photo, again in the railway station, reminds those taking a holiday to remember to come back for the important celebrations. We wonder if the lady holding the baby at the ticket booth is a local, and if so, would she have time to join in what Blackburn had planned for mum's dad's and children?

This page: This was 1951 the year of the Festival of Britain when the nation celebrated its achievements. It was seen as an antidote to the postwar blues and austerity that beset the land. However, Blackburn had its own personal sense of pride to cheer about in 1951. It was the town's centenary of being created a borough. Barney's Band, obviously fuelled on petroleum spirit, played its mixture of oompah and early skiffle. The washboard, kitchen sink and more traditional instruments blended well

enough, surprisingly. Elsewhere, Harry Westwell, winner of the cycling hill climb, took a well-earned rest on Shear Brow, to the north of the town centre. The crowds were so large, as they were the following year for this event, that the police would not allow subsequent climbs to be authorised. Down on King William Street, the Town Hall was well dressed, just as it had been six years earlier during the jollities held to mark the end of the Second World War. The formal creation of the borough came about when the town was amalgamated with Darwen, part of Turton and a clutch of neighbouring villages. It was on 28 August, 1851, that Queen Victoria signed the official charter and William Henry Hornby was elected as the first Mayor of Blackburn. A statue to his memory stands outside the old Town Hall. The municipal building, created in an Italian renaissance style, was built in 1856. It was remodelled in 1969 when a tower block extension, known as 'the new town hall', was added.

'Beating the boundaries', or 'bounds', is a traditional activity that has a throwback to British village life in Anglo Saxon times. Maps were rare and, often on Ascension Thursday, parishioners would mark the limits of church lands so that the information could be passed on to successive generations. This was achieved by walking the boundaries. In time, this became a festive custom with parochial officials heading groups of boys who beat at boundary markers with branches of willow and the like. These children were often given 'the bumps' to help them remember where they had been! The ceremony was revived for the centenary celebrations in 1951 and marked by Mayor W Hare who met some of the 'beaters' at the Town Hall.

Pictured in this group of photographs taken during the Borough's centenary celebrations are a handful of the best floats seen during the parade around the town. Henry Shutt's wagon was parked up outside his premises on Weir Street, off Darwen Street. This company operated a thriving business, with another corn mill in Preston. It provided livestock foods to many north west outlets. The pensioners on another lorry back attracted amusement from the crowds that lined the streets as the procession wound its way along. There were a few ribald comments made, but it was all taken in good spirit. Some of the floats contained tableaux dedicated to the town's industrial heritage. After all, a shuttle is included in our coat of arms, paying homage to the debt the town owes to the humble, but oh so important, piece of textile technology that helped revolutionise the industry and provide the basis for Blackburn's prosperity.

Perhaps it came as something of a surprise that one of the classes was won by this model of a motor boat. Adorned with Players Please slogans to assist the naval theme, it might have been a fine piece of craftsmanship but seemed to have little to do with Blackburn and its past. To name the boat 'Excellent' before judging took place was also somewhat presumptuous, said some.

Above: This image from 1967 depicts part of the fancy dress competition that year. Pity the poor judge who had to choose between contestants whose mums had spent hours making costumes and ensuring that their children had scrubbed up well.

Top right: The Space 71 exhibit at the Agricultural Show was obviously very popular. It had only been a couple of years earlier that Armstrong and Aldrin made the first ever moon landing. In the summer that this mock-up of a space capsule appeared, Scott and Irwin were the astronauts who spent two days going walkabout up there. Remarkably, the eleventh and twelfth and, so far, last men on the moon were Cernan and Schmitt in late 1972. We all expected there to be a McDonald's up there by now!

Right: This was a big occasion for Westholme School in August 1970. Margaret Thatcher visited the school to talk to the girls, possibly about the fact that women can achieve whatever they want to, given the right determination and work ethic. She was Education Secretary at the time and as such would tour schools all over the country. It was Edward Heath who had appointed her to the position and in 1975 she defeated him in the Conservative Party leadership election, later becoming the Prime Minister in 1979. The photograph certainly provides an engaging picture with the often intense Thatcher deep in the detail of needle work, unusual for a qualified chemist and barrister, but the school girls were enjoying the experience and maybe taught her a thing or two. Little did they know at the time that she was to become the longest serving Prime Minister of the 20th Century and the only woman Prime Minister to date.

Getting About

Above: Preparations for a ride in a hot air balloon were almost complete. However, it took nerves of steel to become an intrepid aviator back in the 1880s. Presumably, this occasion, with its large turnout of spectators, was linked with the celebrations being held to mark the golden jubilee of the woman who acceded to the British throne in 1837. Queen Victoria reigned during one of the greatest periods in our history when we had an empire that covered the furthest reaches of the world. However, in her era we still relied on ships rather than hot air balloons to get us there.

Top right and right: The ancient tricycle, dating from 1898, is a real museum piece. To modern eyes, it looks quaint. Contrast that with the bicycles we see outside Cordingley's Cycle Depot. But for the way the men are dressed, those knights of the road, Bradley Wiggins and Chris Hoy, would not seem out of place astride the saddle of any of the machines on display. Yet, the cycle depot was photographed over a century ago, in 1910. Situated on

Blackburn Road, Haslingden, next to the Black Bull Hotel, D T Law's delicatessen and butcher's shop can be found there today. John Cordingley founded Croft Cycle Works in 1882, not far from here on Higher Deardengate.

The Blackburn and Over Darwen Tramways Company (BODTC) was authorised in 1879. Six steam trams from Kitson and Company were purchased to inaugurate the service. These had a seating capacity of 20 in the lower saloon with 26 other passengers accommodated on the top deck. From 1881, steam (top left) and actual horse power (above) offered locals the chance of public transport routes from the centre of Blackburn through Ewood, Earcroft, Hawkshaw and into Darwen at Whitehall. The company was taken over by and split between Blackburn and Darwen Corporations in 1898 and steam trams continued in service until 1901. Work had begun in 1899 to electrify the lines and this process was completed in 1903. By then, Blackburn had 48 double decker and 13 single decker cars. Motor buses were not introduced until the end of the 1920s, but they soon grew in popularity. Although one tram route was abandoned in 1935, plans had been made to extend the service. However, these were put on hold with the outbreak of war in 1939. Track and fleet maintenance suffered during the early 1940s and trams were soon marked out for redundancy. The last car clanked along its line in September 1949. No 49 attracted a sentimental crowd of onlookers as it made its final journey from the Boulevard to Intack Depot. The steam powered and horse driven trams both date from 1895. The more modern No 63 was one of those powered by electricity. This closed top car was passing Mason's Blankets on Church Street in 1910, heading for the Borough Boundary, Darwen.

Above: The motor car in the early years of last century was an item afforded only by the wealthy families in Blackburn. One such family was the Jepsons, who had a family business which dated back to 1870 selling and repairing sewing machines. This had developed a further strand through Richard Jepson, a renowned cycle racer, with a cycle repair shop and motor car spares. The company progressed even further into electrical and furniture items at the large Nova Scotia Mills in Blackburn. Clearly a forward thinking family, Richard had initially owned a steam car when they were first available but here we see the family in a petrol driven car around 1912.

Left: The barge had made its way from the western end of the Leeds-Liverpool Canal, arriving at Whitebirk in April 1945. With the war virtually at an end, eyes were turning towards peace. Women had filled many traditional male roles in the workplace over the previous few years and many looked ahead to continuing using skills they had gained. Not every member of the so-called weaker sex wished to become a mere housewife or to stand aside and surrender jobs in which they had excelled. This group on board the Venus were getting instruction in knot tying as part of their training as bargees.

Above: By 1955, we were starting to leave the austerity blues behind. To use and adapt a mixture of clichés, we had not quite turned the economic corner, but there was light at the end of the financial tunnel. Some of us were able to afford holidays that broke with tradition. The seaside boarding house with its bossy landlady was still popular with many, but others looked further afield for something a little different and the sort of holiday that put us in charge, for a change. Trips to the Continent were not affordable just yet, but a caravan might just fit the bill and let us get off into the countryside or the coast, whichever our fancy favoured. The Caravan Rally in Witton Park, held as part of the investiture celebrations for the new mayor, Alderman Houghton Johnson, gave caravan owners and potential buyers the chance to see these holiday homes on wheels at close quarters.

Left: Blackburn Railway Station was a busy time on weekdays particular at 5.10pm as suggested by the station clock. It was a hive of activity and the drivers of double decker buses certainly needed their wits about them, given the intermingling of cars, wagons and passengers. There may have been one or two families returning from a day trip to Blackpool, which at the time of the photo would have cost the equivalent of 17p for a return ticket. Double deckers were always popular for local advertisers as they provided a travelling billboard to both passengers and pedestrians alike. It could have been Sunol, Glendower Tea Tips or Woodbine Cigarettes that were displayed on the side of the bus, but whatever was being promoted it helped to pay for at least some of the running costs of the bus companies.

Above: Most local Blackburn bus drivers could be said to be well trained and fully conversant with their routes, aware of any difficult bends or bad road surfaces. However, the driver of this bus in Little Harwood in 1969 clearly had mis-calculated the height of the railway bridge or maybe he was a regular single decker driver who had been asked to take on a different route and vehicle. Given the position of the roof and the distance travelled by the remainder of the bus, it must have been travelling at some speed to cause this amount of damage. Whatever the reason for this disastrous accident, the result was dramatic with the roof of a Corporation bus lodged vertically beneath a railway bridge. Amazingly, no-one was seriously hurt, with the only injury being to a lady who was, in fact, on the top deck, but who was able to walk to the surgery for assistance. You have to wonder what happened to the driver?

The weather generally affects transport first and we know well enough about the extensive flooding that has occurred across the country in recent times. But look back to 1964 when Blackburn and Darwen had their own flooding problems. Blackburn Road, in Darwen, became almost impassable in July 1964 but the driver of the Leyland double deck bus was determined to deliver his passengers around Blackburn. And not the holiday this lady in the top left image was hoping for as the floods cut through the annual Wakes Week break for those in Princess Street. Pictured right shows another rescue, this time for a seven-year-old boy who had no doubt thought the floods were amusing until he saw the real problems in his own home. The Fire brigade and Police had been mobilised to help out flood victims from across the affected areas and as these images show, even the sergeants were keen to lend a hand!

Right and below: Horse and carts seemed to remain a preferred means of transport for some for much longer than would have been thought. Motor vehicles were becoming more affordable and available, but a few die-hards would cling on to the romance and novelty of carrying out their daily work in a more traditional way. There is more to this photograph than you may first think. It was taken in 1957, as the horse, Cyrabel and its owner had been taken to court for speeding

in Blackburn. The driver was relieved when the case was thrown out as a speeding horse could not be prosecuted in the same way as a motorist so he probably set off home at a similar speed. Others would carry out their daily work directly from the cart. Do you remember the rag and bone men, and coal merchants who would tread the streets throughout the day? Another tradesman specific to Blackburn was the owner of the 'potato cart', which had an oven at the back in which jacket potatoes would be heated and kept warm for sale to locals and passers by. Ivy Rossi was an early vendor of potatoes from such a cart back in the 1940s and was often found on the Boulevard. Sadly, this unique type of cart is no longer seen in Blackburn having been replaced by the odd, burger and hotdog stall.

Above: The more innovative Blackburnians would find a away to get around in any conditions and this chap was no exception. With skis and poles he was making his way across town just down from the Lord Nelson pub on Penney Street in 1963. The policeman on point duty almost blends in to the snowy backdrop in his white coat and gloves, which were intended to make him more conspicuous to drivers, not less.

It was not until 1929 that an organised Corporation bus service was introduced in Blackburn. Half a dozen each of Leyland single deck Tigers and Leyland double deck Titans were purchased and were initially seen as augmenting the fleet of trams rather than eventually becoming replacements. Both types of transport operated in harness with one another over the next 20 years.

In 1930, powers were sought to enable the running of a fleet of trolleybuses. This would have seen the replacement of tramways in the borough and neighbouring Oswaldtwistle and Church. However, the scheme was not implemented and trolleybuses never

appeared on our streets. So, when the tramways were pulled up in 1949, 83 new motorbuses were purchased, doing away

with the need for any more to be purchased until the late 1950s. Following changes caused by local government reorganisation in 1974, the mainly olive green and ivory coachwork of the buses gave way to a combination of green, white and red. For the best part of a decade they were known as the 'Italian flag' buses, but a return to the traditional livery was made in 1983, much to the approval of most of us. The oldest of the accompanying photos (top left) shows The Boulevard in the 1930s. The single decker in the foreground of this image was operated by Ribble, a Preston bus company founded in 1919. Its poppy red livery brightened up many northwest town centres. The scene looking down upon The Boulevard was snapped in 1955, while the images on this page date from the mid 1960s.

A Working Life

Above: There was a huge growth in motor vehicles around the towns and cities of the north and Blackburn was no exception. The roads around the 1930s were filled with a mix of trams, carts, bicycles, wagons and, of course, cars. It was this blend of traffic on the roads and the increasing power and speed of vehicles that had lead to an increase in death and injuries. There had been over 4,800 deaths on the road since 1926. This inevitably lead to government intervention in the form of the Road Traffic Act of 1930. Strangely enough, this new Act included a provision for the abolition of speed restrictions on UK roads. All of this had lead to the implementation of the Police Motor Patrol we see here in Blackburn in 1931. These three vehicles would have been able to reach accidents quickly, stop and arrest offenders and ensure pedestrians were made aware of the dangers of the road. Are the two chaps looking on, the proud inspector and police sergeant perhaps?

Right: A few decades later, the police representatives stand upright for a photograph in Witton Park, Blackburn, in 1962. They have the Bedford ' black mariah' behind, which would have been used for transporting criminals from crime scene to the police station, and from there to the courts. Women in the police had a serious role to play at the time and most forward thinking forces would have ensured they had a good number in their ranks. Traffic patrol by motor scooter had become popular particularly around busy towns and the Sixties saw a real growth in scooter ownership with the introduction of the Italian models, such as the Vespa and Lambretta. They were generally cheap to run, easy to park and for the 'Mods' of the day in their 'Parkers', Crombie coats and smart suits they were the defining mode of transport which set them aprt from the motorbike riding 'Rockers'.

Left and below: It wasn't just motor patrols and criminals that occupied the police of Blackburn. There were times when their planning and manpower had to be used for the wider community benefit. Here we see five 'bobbies' taking food sacks out to the cut-off community of Tockholes in March 1955 following heavy snows. It was the only way the locals could receive provisions until the snow cleared a little. The bread patrol we see making their way through the snow are a wider collection of service people and include ambulance, police, firemen and civilians, all willing to help with deliveries to the older and the isolated families in the area.

Right: There are lots of smiling faces in this photograph and no wonder. It was that community spirit once more which brought children from major cities of the north to more rural towns to escape the bombings of the Second World War. These evacuees and the ladies and helpers who would be taking them into their homes are seen on Blackburn Station in 1940. We can see the small bags of belongings each child was allowed and the mandatory gas masks in the square box containers, slung over the shoulders of many of the children. The people of Blackburn would always rally around to help out. And who's left holding the baby? Well it's the local Bobby, of course, and he looks pretty happy about it too!

Facing page: With greater prosperity after the war came the desire for more comfortable homes. Carpets were one of the ways that old floors could be covered, draughts limited and a warm and cosy feel could be brought to the previously austere home. Blackburn's part in the carpet industry was significant in that tufting machinery was made to high precision in the town. The concept had been developed in the US by the Cobble brothers and with access to Europe, a willing and recession hit workforce and no language barriers, the UK was a prime place to build new machinery manufacturing workshops. At first, machines were shipped from America by Cobble, who had set up a subsidiary in Blackburn, but later machines were manufactured in Blackburn to the American design. In this photo from the late 1950s we see one of the women workers overseeing a lock stitching machine wearing the 'uniform' of the day, the flower printed overall smock.

Left: Another staple commodity from the clothing manufacturing side of Blackburn was the shoe industry and Newman's was a forerunner. Newman's Footwear Ltd was founded by Walter Newman who owned a large shoe factory in Germany before the war. Having fled Germany and being almost penniless he chose to establish a new footwear company in Blackburn due to it already having a small shoe and slipper industry. At one time the company employed 700 people and true to the Newman's philosophy, all staff and their partners, plus dignitaries, were invited to celebrate Christmas at King George's Hall. Over 1,600 guests enjoyed Newman's splendid hospitality. Pictured is the shoe assembly line the early days.

ndustry in Blackburn was indeed broad and varied and it was no surprise that the Second World War drove crucial industries to the safer areas of the north west away from the bombings across London and the south. Aviation was no exception and with English Electric identified for the the building and assembly of heavy bombers and aircraft, Blackburn and Preston became the hub of this industry. Associated suppliers also joined the war efort to maintain a reliable flow of components. The focus for aircraft construction

was in Samlesbury on a site which had been previously earmarked for a civil airport feeding Blackburn and Preston. It was vital work for the people of Blackburn and critical to the war effort with the first hanger being completed in October 1940. These workers would be kept busy with orders for 200 Halifax MkII bombers and later over 2,500 De Havilland Vampires. Other aircraft assembled here included the Hampden and Canberra planes. Top left we can see work in progress with the installation of the heavy engine on the giant Halifax bomber. The importance of the site and operations within is shown in the bottom left image with VIPs and dignitaries visiting the major Halifax assembly line in Shed 2 in 1940, standing beneath a huge Lancaster bomber.

A fascinated crowd gathered on Railway Road in 1963 to view work taking place on the new Blakewater culvert. The dry weather channel in the centre was intended to keep the waters flowing when the river level was low, so cutting down on the amount of silting up that might otherwise take place. The photographer perched himself precariously on the jib of a large crane to get his shot from above. The work being done was also part of the redevelopment scheme that included the building of a new market and hall. The original culverting took place during the industrial revolution. It now runs under Ainsworth Street and between the bus station and cathedral.

Ainsworth Jewellers
A Sparkling History

From time immemorial humans have valued jewellery. The most primitive of our distant ancestors made necklaces and body ornaments. In later ages gold and silver, together with precious stones, were combined by skilled artisans. We still value jewellery.

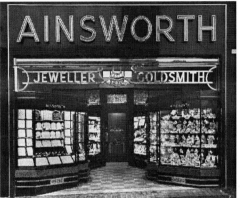

The name of Ainsworth Jewellers is well known in Blackburn – and so it should be, for the firm has been in existence since the reign of Queen Victoria. In fact A Ainsworth & Sons (Jewellers) Ltd is Blackburn's oldest established town centre retailer.

The business was established in 1870 by Joseph Ainsworth – the great grandfather of one of the current directors, Philip Ainsworth, himself the son of the other current director Kenneth Ainsworth.

Today, the business is located at 57-59 Darwen Street.

Originally, however, the family firm was located at the top end of Darwen Street at number 9A, but in 1885 Joseph moved to 12 Northgate, subsequently also occupying No. 15.

In 1907, Joseph, now joined by his three sons Alf, James and George, purchased 48 Market Place.

Later, George's son Arnold came into the business, working at Market Place. Following some thirty years at the property next door, it was at 50 Market Place, acquired in 1938, that the business really prospered, and where it would remain until 1965.

By the early 1960s, Arnold's two sons, Michael and Kenneth, had both joined him at Market Place. Kenneth's son Philip joined the firm in 1990. Michael Ainsworth retired from the business in 1995.

During the massive changes that were to affect the town centre in the redevelopment of the 1960s, Ainsworth's knocked 57 and 59 Darwen Street into one to create two floors of showroom selling fine jewellery and watches, clocks and giftware. Most, if not all, locals will have heard of and experienced the special Ainsworth Jewellers service that has become associated with this long-established family business.

Today, as ever, the company is proud of its Blackburn roots, its friendly and professional service and its ability to cater for the families of Blackburn and for those extra special business or social presentations, in addition to its highly-regarded repair and valuation service.

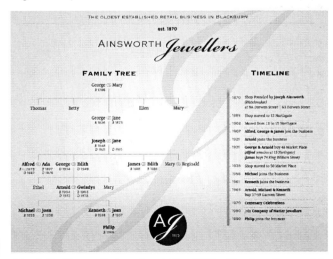

*Top left: Ainsworth Jewellers in the 1930s. **Centre:** Ainsworth's 50 Market Place premises in 1956. **Left:** A Ainsworth & Sons 57-59 Darwen Street in1964. **Above:** Ainsworth Jewellers family tree and company timeline.*

Blackburn College
Inspiring, Innovating & Achieving Together

Education is important in every society, but few communities have valued education as highly as the residents of Blackburn. And in the closing decades of Queen Victoria's long reign, the demand for educational opportunities reached a new high.

For more than 125 years Blackburn College, now Pennine Lancashire's largest post-sixteen education provider, has been meeting the educational and training needs of the area's industry and commerce, as well as other sectors of the community. In 2007, the College was declared 'outstanding' by Ofsted and in 2008 it was awarded a Beacon Award for its excellence in teaching and learning. The College is consequently among the top five per cent of all Learning and Skills Council funded providers.

Today, the College offers a wide range of courses - from A Levels to Apprenticeships and Vocational courses in Hair and Beauty, Childhood Studies, Public Services, Construction, Music, Media and Textiles, through to Foundation Degrees, Degrees, Masters and Professional Qualifications.

The idea of founding Blackburn College is attributed to two local men. One of them, W.E. Bickerdike, was a manufacturing chemist in Oswaldtwistle; he had a particular interest in technical education after seeing it at work in Germany in the early 1870s.

Whilst visiting Berlin in 1872, Bickerdike was impressed by the importance that was attached to scientific instruction there, something which was in marked contrast to the relative indifference displayed towards teaching science in England.

Bickerdike's early attempts to enthuse local people with the idea of opening a college in Blackburn initially fell on deaf ears. Many local businessmen were opposed to the provision of education for the working classes and felt that enough was already supplied by the Mechanics' Institute and various private colleges.

Above: The empty site on Blakey Moor in 1887. **Below:** *The Technical College, completed in 1894.*

W.E. Bickerdike's luck changed, however, when he joined forces with the Mayor at that time, Edgar Appleby, and linked the venture with the forthcoming Golden Jubilee of Queen Victoria in 1887.

The idea for a college caught on, and prominent local people soon became involved in the organisation and, more importantly, the financing of the project. A subscription list was opened, and about £15,000 was given voluntarily to build the school. Edgar Appleby, the Mayor, made substantial personal donations to the fund and stood for office a second time in order to see the project through.

A suitable site was chosen on Blakey Moor and building work commenced on this major undertaking. May 9th, 1888, marked two milestones in the history of Blackburn. Firstly, it was the day of the first ever Royal Visit to the town. Thousands of local people gathered to catch a glimpse of the Prince and Princess of Wales; memories of the occasion would be recounted for many years to come.

The future King and Queen were transported along Preston New Road in the State Carriage flanked by mounted Lancers in their immaculate uniforms.

The second milestone was, of course, the laying of the foundation stone for Blackburn's first public college, and the start of an era of opportunity for ordinary people based upon merit and achievement. The actual laying of the stone was done within a huge marquee.

Inside the foundation stone was placed a bottle containing coins, local newspapers and an inscription on vellum. Afterwards, the Prince of Wales was made the first Honorary Freeman of the Borough of Blackburn. There followed a grand lunch in the Town Hall at which the Prince spoke about his support for the concept of technical education and its importance to the success of manufacturing industry. The Prince and Princess of Wales left during the afternoon, whilst local people continued to celebrate into the night with a fireworks display in Corporation Park.

In 1891, three years after the laying of the foundation stone, the first students moved into the building. Work was almost complete by that time. A wide range of subjects was taught, including Chemistry, Art, Building and Physics; particular emphasis, however, was placed on Textiles and Engineering.

Many of the classes were held in the evenings after most of the students had completed their day's work in the local mills and factories. The courses were accessible to everyone, but were not free. A fee of ten shillings (50p), a substantial sum in those days, was required in advance from students as a minimum payment for participation at this new seat of learning.

Soon afterwards, financial assistance came from Blackburn Council, which was to be involved in the running of the College from that time on.

The first couple of decades were difficult in terms of the organisation and running of the College. The result, in 1903, was that the College was taken over by Blackburn Education Committee and renamed Blackburn Municipal Technical School. By 1909, there were only 50 day-time students, but a massive 1,300 evening students attended the school. The evening classes were largely attended by apprentices from local businesses.

This page: 1940s views in the Weaving Shed (top left), typewriting class (above) and woodwork class (below).

In 2003, work began on an extension to the original Victoria Building on Blakey Moor. Work on the New Victoria Building was completed in 2005 and officially opened by the Queen's cousin, the Duke of Gloucester.

The new extension cost £4.4 million and created specialist teaching facilities for the College's Hair and Beauty, Hospitality and Business departments, including a 120-seater student-run restaurant – 'Scholars' - and state-of-the-art hair and beauty salons.

Meanwhile, it had become apparent that a large part of the College was no longer fit for purpose, and in September 2007 the first phase of the College's multi-million pound Master Plan to create a new world-class campus was opened.

Progress continued over the years, and by 1950 there were 4,000 students on the roll of what was by now the Blackburn Municipal Technical College and School of Art. Soon it became clear that more room was needed to accommodate the growing number of students. New buildings were commissioned and the foundation stone was laid by Lord Derby in 1954, in a large area between Nab Lane and Montague Street. The Feilden Street buildings were constructed in three phases between 1953 and 1963, and officially opened in 1964 by Lord Robens.

The textile industry dominated the town for many years, but as that industry contracted, the study of textile manufacturing disappeared from the College syllabus. In the mid-1960s, the name was changed to Blackburn College of Technology and Design, but when the College became the main provider of tertiary education in the borough in 1984, it was shortened to the more familiar Blackburn College.

In June 1988, when the College celebrated its centenary, the highlight of the year was the visit from His Royal Highness the Prince of Wales. He came to the College and removed the bottle from the foundation stone which his great-great grandfather had placed there a hundred years before. The contents were intact despite rumours that the coins had been stolen by workmen during the construction of the Victoria Building. A 'time capsule' to represent 1988 was prepared by local school children and placed inside the stone by Prince Charles.

The £8.8 million St Paul's Centre now houses the two areas of The Sixth Form and I.T. Phase two – the £14 million University Centre – was opened in 2009 and further phases included the demolition of the existing Feilden Street building, sympathetic

Top left: *Pictured in 1956 from the roof of the Feilden Street Building is St Paul's Gardens and the site of what is now the new University Centre.* **Left:** *The new Technology Centre in 1988 which at the time had the most up-to-date computing facilities.* **Top right:** *Prince Charles' visit to Blackburn College during Centenary Year, 1988.* **Above:** *The new University Centre by night.*

refurbishment of the Old Victoria building which was upgraded with a new roof, windows and structural work as well as updates to the Creative Arts Centre.

2013 saw the official opening of the Sir Bill Taylor Futures Centre, dedicated to STEM (Science, Technology, Engineering and Maths) and was built to fill the high level STEM skills gap in Pennine Lancashire.

Looking forward, Blackburn College will see the opening of the state-of-the-art Regional Automotive Centre in September 2014. It has been developed with input from leading manufacturers Nissan and Skoda, and contains the latest equipment and technology to deliver the skills the industry needs in the 21st Century.

The £13.5 million Blackburn Sport and Leisure Centre, built collaboratively by Blackburn College and Blackburn with Darwen Council, will also open the doors to the first phase in September 2014, culminating in the grand opening in January 2015 where both students and locals will be able to access outstanding facilities including a training pool and health suite.

From modest beginnings the College now provides learning opportunities to over 15,000 students of all ages and backgrounds and is connected with more than 4,000 employers, locally and regionally.

Today, in the 21st century, Blackburn College campus has physically changed beyond recognition since it was founded in the reign of Queen Victoria, yet, crucially, the overriding aim of being the prime provider of the community's educational and cultural needs, in support of employment remains unaltered.

Top: The Beacon Centre, 2014. **Above:** Interior views of the University Centre (left) and the Beacon Centre. **Bottom left:** The Regional Automotive Hub opening in September 2014. **Below:** Bill Taylor, chair of governors, outside the Sir Bill Taylor Futures Centre.

CSH Transport & Forwarding Ltd

CSH Transport & Forwarding Ltd is a privately owned client-focused logistics company operating in three key areas - dry freight, liquid bulk and specialist chemical transportation. Based at Sett End Road North, on Blackburn's Shadsworth Business Park, it operates nationally throughout the UK and the European Union, 24/7, 365 days a year.

From humble beginnings, with just one truck, the company now has a full range of vehicles, with in excess of fifty trailers and tractor units that carry everything from hazardous and non-hazardous chemicals, some of which are essential to our daily lives, to engineering components and microscopic computing and automotive products.

CSH's focus from the outset was on providing a professional transport service that is tailored to its clients' needs with a friendly and flexible service to give existing and future clients an excellent and sustainable logistics partner. CSH Transport has benefited throughout its past thirty years from the enthusiasm of its founder, Stuart Haworth. A strong history as a competitive sportsman, combined with his environmental awareness and social ethics, have proved strong assets over the years.

Stuart Haworth founded the firm in 1979 with the help of his father Harry Haworth.

Stuart worked in engineering, serving his time as a toolmaker at Platt Saco Lowell, formerly Howard & Bulloughs, in Accrington. On turning 20 years of age Stuart was made redundant. He stayed in engineering, and worked at Lucas Industries, in Accrington. In 1979, the Year of Discontent, Stuart was about to be made redundant again, so he decided to go into Transport with his father's help.

Transport is what Stuart really always wanted to do.

When he was growing up Stuart's father was a major influence because he was always involved in transport, from being a driver to becoming a transport manager and then running his own Forwarding company.

Top left: Founder, Stuart Haworth and wife Christine. **Above:** *CSH's original premises on Alan Ramsbottom way in Great Harwood.* **Below and facing page:** *Vehicles from the CSH fleet of the 1990s and 2000s.*

Initially, CSH moved to Blackburn's Whitebirk Industrial Estate, which gave the firm more room to expand, plus full maintenance facilities. By then, in the late 1990s, the company had expanded to employ around 30 staff. The products carried to Europe were mainly automotive-related, to factories like Volvo, Sweden, Jeep in Linz, Austria, and also raw materials into related factories in Belgium and Italy.

Also in the 1990s, CSH provided a 'groupage' service for various customers to France, Germany and the Benelux countries. By 2000, this part of the business had started to slow down, but UK work picked up. CSH took the decision in 2001 to stop delivering palletised goods outside mainland UK. The only job that kept going was a tanker delivery to a factory approximately 100 miles inland from Barcelona, Spain, delivering scented oil.

Stuart and his father, Harry, started by operating a number of box vans working on a contract, mainly acting as an agent; doing that enabled them to put a deposit down on a 7.5 ton gvw vehicle in May 1980. Their first vehicle was a Magirus Deutz flatback. Once the vehicle was bought, Stuart drove it for the initial few years, subcontracting work from his father.

When the business started, Stuart operated it mainly from his home. After some six years, Christine, Stuart's wife, became involved doing the office work and answering the phone while Stuart drove. Christine, Stuart and Harry's initials provided the company name. By then the firm had four vehicles and was employing its own drivers.

Still maintaining its steady growth, by 2005 CSH realised more space was needed, so Stuart started to look around for premises. When a customer decided to sell its premises in Blackburn - a five-acre site at Shadsworth - this was bought by CSH. The head office and the palletised goods operation were moved to the new site at Shadsworth whilst keeping hold of the Whitebirk site for the firm's Tanker Division and the maintenance facility.

By 2005, the tanker operation had changed. With the decline in the paper industry the opportunity came to sub-contract dedicated tanker work from a company in Yorkshire. This work went well, and slowly CSH stopped doing most of the paper related deliveries and went totally over to chemical distribution using dedicated tankers.

In the 1980s, a lot of work was automotive or chemical related; and then in the early 1990s the firm was asked by BTR to do work into mainland Europe. This included driving to Austria, Sweden, Belgium, Italy and Spain.

In March 1997, CSH was asked by an existing customer to take his tanker business on board, which proved initially successful. But with the decline of the paper industry CSH changed to carrying specialist chemicals on dedicated tankers.

Originally located in Clayton-le-Moors, the firm later moved to Great Harwood, and witnessed significant growth in the company. The move to Blackburn has, however, shown the best results, giving CSH the opportunity to grow and offer warehousing and other related services to customers.

After a few years Jack and Hazel Adams, from whom CSH was subcontracting, asked Stuart if he would be interested in buying them out. An agreement was made and CSH continues to do that work today. Unfortunately, Jack died not long after.

In 2008/9, when the recession started, CSH had one or two client companies go into receivership, but fortunately most are still operating.

The following six years were quite difficult, but CSH has still managed to invest in vehicles and trailers and now employs up to 60 people, CSH Transport tries to give a bespoke delivery service on its own vehicles at a competitive price, either pallet-wise or bulk. The company aims to ensure its customers are fully satisfied with the services provided at all times. In order to achieve that aim CSH relies on the commitment and effectiveness of its employees. It is therefore vital that all work together as a team to achieve the company's goals. Stuart has always said that if an employee at CSH does his best to achieve these goals that is good enough.

A top priority, meanwhile, is continued investment year on year, spending money on both vehicles and trailers. That investment keeps CSH at the forefront of technology, emissions etc. All the vehicles are enabled for tracking and 'telematics'.

CSH has seen steady growth over the past three decades, and the plan is to carry on the path of sustainable growth.

Meanwhile, life for Stuart has not all been about transport in lorries. In 2011, Stuart Haworth undertook a cycle ride from San Francisco to Los Angeles, a six- day pedal covering approximately 550 miles: this was for Leuka, a Leukemia research charity, and he raised £4,950 for the cause. The training made for a quite intense year, but the results were extremely worthwhile.

Top left and above: Two of CSH's dedicated tankers.
Below: A bird's eye view of CSH's Shadsworth Business Park premises, 2014.

The year 2013 saw CSH Transport sponsoring a sculpture of two steel fighting stags called 'Natural Forces in Challenging Times', in conjunction with artist John Everiss and Groundwork, another charitable concern that works closely with the local Council in Blackburn. It initially went on show at Tatton Park Garden Festival but Stuart was keen to find a good permanent home for the work and with Blackburn and Darwen's approval the sculpture has been sited on the roundabout outside the Royal Blackburn Hospital. It is perfectly postioned to welcome visitors from throughout the area and for the people of Blackburn.

Today, CSH's main customer base is general haulage with a chemical bias. All the firm's drivers are fully trained to carry hazardous substances. As well as hazardous and non-hazardous chemicals and standard palletised goods, various other materials are also catered for including such things as flooring for equestrian centres or products used for the manufacture of yacht sails, printing material, raw materials, paper reels and the finished inserts for magazines, papers and the like.

Looking back over more than three decades in the business, Stuart Haworth says: "Haulage was and is always a challenge, it is always competitive, with timed and deadline deliveries, vehicle reliability and driver reliability. However, the great thing is, it's never boring, there is always something new going on whether it's changes to the law or changes in technology. Probably the best thing is the people you work with and the customers and suppliers you meet. We have been fortunate to have customers and employees who have been with us over 20 years and that loyalty has led to friendships. I would like to thank our employees, customers and suppliers for their continued support and loyalty this past 35 years."

Above: The CSH team. Below: A familiar sight to the people of Blackburn and beyond, the new CSH livery on one of the company's latest 2014 plate Volvos.

Educational Printing Services
Live, Lean and Prospering

Now based in Glenfield Park, Northrop Avenue, Blackburn, Educational Printing Services Ltd was founded in January 1975. From a modest start printing tickets for local shows and concerts, the founder and his colleagues started to tour education exhibitions where they had the idea for Exercise Books thus expanding the business. The company at present produces nearly two million standard and bespoke exercise books a year. As well as exercise books, the company also produces other educational resources such as pupil booklets, pupil diaries and planners, and school reports etc. that can be personalised to enhance a school's image.

The founder of the company was Frederick Henry Pickering. He was a teacher but decided he wanted to do something different, even though everyone told him not to do so!

Fred Pickering decided that if he tried and it didn't work he could go back to teaching. As he started the business his wife had just left teaching to have their first baby – who was born on 16th February, 1975, just one month after the new venture began. The long-term future of the new business was, however, a long way from being certain.

The year 1975 was far from being an auspicious one to start a new business. Economically Britain was being dubbed 'the sick man of Europe'. Under Harold Wilson's Labour Government inflation was rampant, reaching a peak approaching 25%. Industrial strife, strikes and walkouts caused daily inconveniences. The previous year had seen the notorious three-day week, with power cuts leading to candles and oil lamps very much back in use. Coal miners finally gave up industrial action after being given a 35% pay award from the Government.

An event of greatest significance, though one not perceived as such at the time, came on 11th February, 1975, when the little-known Margaret Thatcher defeated Edward Heath in the Conservative Party leadership election to become the party's first female leader. Mrs Thatcher, 49, had previously been Education Secretary in the Heath government from 1970 to 1974.

Despite the daunting economic times the founder of Educational Printing Services was a very determined man, and one who worked long and hard to make the business succeed. Fred Pickering bought a rundown printing business on Whalley Banks and called the business 'Whalley Graphics' – a name which was later changed to 'Educational Printing Services Limited' because he printed mainly for education.

Top left: Founder, Frederick Henry Pickering. **Left:** *Where it all began, EPS's first premises.* **Below:** *The company's former Higher Audley Street works.*

The premises were on three levels and very difficult to manage – but Fred did manage them. Initially Fred and two other men started working for the company with a single old style Platen Letterpress.

Fred not only ran the business but also did a lot of deliveries himself – sometimes leaving home at three in the morning to deliver to schools in London, and then coming back to the north and doing a full day's work. Hard work and commitment to developing the business would eventually bring their due reward.

The company also used to print season tickets and programmes for Blackburn Rovers Football Club and carry out various other works for Chelsea and Reading Football Clubs.

Fred and his wife, Glenis, often had to wait for their wages because they didn't have enough money. They had no computers at first, and all work was done on old-fashioned typewriters. Wages were paid in cash. Glenis often took the money to the bank as there were not many cheques.

Eventually, the firm moved to other premises in the centre of Blackburn before moving to Higher Audley Street. In December, 1993, it moved to Water Street in Great Harwood with factory space of 32,000 sq. ft. Later, Fred and his colleagues started to tour education exhibitions where they had the idea for Exercise Books thus expanding the business.

In April, 1999, Fred's son, David, started in the business, having already done holiday jobs there beforehand. Glenis was Company Secretary and a Director in the beginning (and is still Company Secretary).

*Top: Educational Printing Services' Albion Mill factory in Water Street, Great Harwood. **Left:** Fred and his wife Glenis. **Above:** Fred and son David, the current owner of Educational Printing Services Ltd.*

Educational Printing Services Limited started publishing for the education sector in 2000, providing a wide range of teachers' resources and pupil resources in almost every school subject from foundation to secondary schools.

David took over the running of Educational Printing Services Limited from his father Fred in 2002. David is involved in all aspects of the business in an advisory and organisational role. David plans and directs the company's activities to achieve targets and standards for financial and trading performance, quality and legislative adherence. He also oversees the company's functions and performance via the executive team.

Almost a decade later, 2010 saw another move, this time to Blackburn where the premises now extend to 48,000 sq. ft.

Intriguingly, Educational Printing Services operates from the same site as the famous British Northrop Loom Co Ltd once did.

British Northrop was one of Blackburn's most successful companies, established in 1902 to build textile looms designed by J. H. Northrop, of Hopedale, USA. The Northrop Automatic Loom was revolutionary in its time. It used a rotating magazine to keep the shuttle constantly supplied with cotton thread and could be run 24 hours a day, stopping itself automatically when threads broke, thus negating the need for skilled weavers unlike in times past where they were essential. The role of the weaver was changed forever; they could now tend more looms – meaning fewer were employed in mills. New Northrop factories were built in Blackburn before and after WWI – by the 1950s Northrop employed over 3,000 operatives, producing an average of 10,000 looms a year. These were exported across the globe and had a huge impact on developing third world economies. In fact, the worldwide success of the Northrop Automatic Loom contributed directly to the rapid post-war decline of Lancashire's own cotton industry. Happily nature abhors a vacuum: Norththrop and the textile industry's loss would eventually become EPS's gain.

Today, Educational Printing Services Limited promotes its products and services to nearly 30,000 schools nationwide. Customers include not only schools but also City Councils, School and Public Library Services, Buying Groups, Wholesalers and Retailers, International Publishers, Office Supply Companies and Stationers.

EPRINT Publishing, the publishing division of Educational Printing Services Limited, provides a wide range of teacher and pupil resources in almost every school subject from foundation stage through to secondary school. The company has nearly 45 authors who are experienced educational practitioners.

*Top: A view of the warehouse floor with two offset printing machines on the right. **Above**: EPS's Muller stitch liner, capable of producing 24,000 books per day.*

added a fourth division to the company and was able to supply even more schools throughout the UK and abroad with its products.

Back when the company first started, Homework Diaries were the firm's most popular product; they used to be collated by walking round the dining room table in Fred and Glenis' home. Now, the most popular product is exercise books. The firm currently produce over 4 million books per year and has around a 10% market share in the education sector.

EPRINT Publishing also offers a full range of educational materials and resources that run alongside the lesson being taught, for example, rubber stamps, friezes and puppets.

The firm is extremely proud of its Teacher/Parent Resource Books which have been written by qualified teachers and head-teachers and EPS believes the content of its books to be of the highest quality. Its 'Grab & Go' books provide quick resources for teachers and parents to readily use, without the need for reading lengthy introductions. In addition, the growing range of titles for reluctant readers follows the British Dyslexia Association guidelines and provides fascinating and interesting reads to both dyslexia sufferers and disengaged readers.

November 2011 saw the company add a new division, EPS Finishing, which is the print finishing part of the company. Then in February 2012, Educational Printing Services Limited acquired Plural Education, a firm which supplied educational products to Independent schools. With this acquisition the firm

EPS proudly claims that its products are better than those of competitors because of their quality, whilst still being competitively priced. The company also offers a wide range of choice and personalisation options for its exercise books, diaries and reading record books. In terms of machinery the firm now has three vertical tower booklet collators, one saddle stitcher, five offset printers, four black and white digital printers, one colour digital printer, one folding machine and a variety of other finishing machines.

Today, four decades after its founding, Educational Printing Services Ltd is live, lean and prosperous, and looking forward to the future with confidence, whilst looking back on its past with justifiable pride.

Above: The factory in preparation for the peak summer season. *Below:* Educational Printing Services Ltd's Glenfield Park, Northrop Avenue, Blackburn, premises.

QEGS
The Queen of Schools

In 1877, the Elizabethan charter was replaced by a scheme whereby the name of the school was changed to Blackburn Grammar School. The Governing Body now had representative governors from the Town Council and School Board.

The school moved to its present site, half a mile to the west of Blackburn town centre, in 1884. Bounded by West Park Road, Dukes Brow, and the cricket field of the East Lancashire Club, the site has been likened to a small university campus. The school's excellent Harrison Playing Fields are a mile away, at Lammack Road.

In the late 19th century Blackburn Grammar School had fewer than 100 boys on its roll, though many went on to make their mark – John Garstang in archaeology, Sir Harold Derbyshire and Sir Benjamin Ormerod in law, Sir Ernest Marsden in physics and Pomfret Kilner in plastic surgery.

'**D**isce Prodesse', the Latin motto of Queen Elizabeth's Grammar School in Blackburn, translates as 'learn to be of service'. Its pupils have been learning to be of service throughout five centuries.

April 2014 marked the 500th anniversary of the school's Foundation Deed being signed at Lathom Hall, near Ormskirk, the family home of the Earls of Derby.

Queen Elizabeth's, which educates boys and girls from the age of three to eighteen, is a selective 'HMC' school, proud of its ability to prepare pupils not just for university but for life.

In addition to high academic standards, QEGS (as the school is popularly known) offers a wide range of extra-curricular activities that help to produce rounded and confident young men and women.

During the 20th century, the school expanded in numbers, becoming known as 'Queen Elizabeth's Grammar School, Blackburn' in April 1933, during the Headship of Arthur Holden. The Holden science buildings, opened in 1958, are named after him.

Top left: Pupils donning mortar boards pose for the camera at Freckleton Street, circa 1874. *Below left:* The Charter Window at QEGS. *Above:* Former pupil and Headmaster, Arthur Holden. *Below:* Milk distribution outside the old gym, 1950s.

The school was founded as a free grammar school at Blackburn by Thomas Stanley, the 2nd Earl of Derby, and received its Royal Charter from Queen Elizabeth I in 1567.

Beginning modestly as the chantry school to the Parish Church of St Mary the Virgin (now Blackburn Cathedral), the school remained located there until the need to build a new church required the school to move, first to a temporary home in nearby Market Street Lane and then, in 1825, to Bull Meadow, just outside the town. The school building and the adjoining Headmaster's House can still be seen on what is now Freckleton Street.

Her Majesty Queen Elizabeth II opened the new Queen's Wing in 1987; the school's on-site swimming pool and new Sixth Form Centre were opened in the following decade.

In 2001, QEGS became fully co-educational (having welcomed girls into its Sixth Form in 1976) and the following year opened an Early Years section for boys and girls between the ages of three and six.

Now, under Simon Corns, Headmaster since 2007, the school has over 700 pupils.

Many distinguished former pupils have passed through the doors of Queen Elizabeth's in recent decades, not least designer Wayne Hemingway, TV presenter Krishnan Guru-Murthy, music promoter Yvette Livesey and professional golfer Nick Dougherty.

Traditionally strong in science, the school can also point to excellence in Art, Modern Languages, Classics and Mathematics. Drama is always of a high standard, and QEGS is renowned in sport.

The school will operate as a 'Free School' from September 2014.

After 500 years, QEGS continues to educate pupils to the highest academic standards, in accordance with a clear moral code. Redevelopment and improvements are ongoing, as the school continues offering the best possible education and preparation for life. Refurbished facilities for Biology, Mathematics and Complementary Studies where brought into use in 2008, and a new extension to the Sports Hall at the Harrison Playing Fields at Lammack, opened in 2011.

In 2012, the old art block at Brooklands was renovated to become the new nursery school, taking children from three months to four years.

Students being educated at Queen Elizabeth's today keenly follow in the school's tradition, still striving to 'be of service'. The fundraising and practical help given to charities and those in need illustrate clearly the determination to make a difference, which has always been the hallmark of a QEGS student.

*Top left: Presentation of a silver vase to Her Majesty the Queen at the opening of the Queen's Wing in 1987. **Above:** A 2009 bird's eye view of Queen Elizabeth's Grammar School. **Left and above left:** A commemorative plaque (left) for the official opening of the new extension to the Sports Hall (above left) on 24 March, 2011. **Below:** Sixth Form students in Singleton House Sixth Form Centre.*

Ainsworth's Funeral Services
Complete Funeral Services For All Since 1856

It is often said that there are only two certainties in life – death and taxes. Taxes can sometimes be avoided but the end of life is an inevitability. And for those left behind there are many problems to be dealt with, not least arranging a funeral.

In the distant past it was often a simple matter. A local woman did the 'laying out' in one's own home, whilst a local carpenter might make the coffin, which would be left in the front room until the actual day of burial. Over the years matters got more complicated. As result the occupation of professional undertaker arose to help families through those most difficult of times.

For longer than anyone can now remember Ainsworth's Funeral Services have been arranging funerals for many religious denominations and for non-religious families alike. The bespoke service provided is sensitive and respectful, helping clients with every aspect of the funeral arrangements.

The firm which would become Edwin Ainsworth Ltd has been based in Church Bank Street, Darwen, since 1871, but it was originally housed in a row of cottages in Ainsworth Street, which also included stabling for 12 horses. The firm was founded in 1856 by local businessman James Ainsworth, and like many undertakers at the time it was much more than just a funeral service.

James Ainsworth was the local Registrar of Births and Deaths – a fact which no doubt led to the commencement of the funeral business. James himself died in 1877 at the early age of 56 years. His son, Edwin, was left to carry on the business and was blessed with five sons to help him.

Top: Founder, James Ainsworth (left) and his son, Edwin, who the firm was named after. *Left:* A company letterhead from 1900 showing the firm's Church Bank Livery Stables. *Below:* The firm's horse-drawn fleet outside their Church Bank Street, Darwen, premises in the early 1900s.

It was Edwin who truly established the business. Although Edwin, too, died at the early age of 56 years he was by then already known to many by the affectionate name of 'Old Ted'. By then, new premises had been built at Church Bank Street, which became well known as the Boro Mews.

The business also included coachbuilders and joiners, and for many years, as late as 1922, Ainsworth's provided horse buses to Blackburn on market days. Five horses pulled the carriage up the rut covered old lane, though the journey took only 15 minutes to travel from Darwen town centre to Blackburn.

The firm's first motor vehicle, an eight-horse-power Humber car, was bought in 1910 and converted for use as a 'coffin handy', the modern-day equivalent of a hearse. Horses were finally replaced with Rolls Royce cars in 1922. Meanwhile, for forty years, Ainsworth's provided an ambulance service to the former Moss Bridge Hospital until the county ambulance service took over in 1954.

The company was handed down through the Ainsworth family and became Limited in 1931 when James Ainsworth's grandsons, William and Ernest, decided they needed outside help.

Of 'Old Ted's' five sons it was Will and Ernest who played the largest part in the development of the company. Will was the first of the two to retire in 1937. Ernest retired in 1944.

Whilst the main business would always be funeral directing the taxi service continued to be an important part of the firm's activities until private ownership of cars became commonplace. There can be few Darwen families who at some time did not use Ainsworth's taxis for weddings, parties and other social events.

Though no longer in the taxi business, the firm still provides limousines for funerals which can take up to seven passengers. And in an echo of the early days it even offers a complete horse drawn funeral with a team of two, four or six black or white horses, with black or white carriage.

There have been many Directors since Will and Ernest Ainsworth retired; the present ones, Gregory and Patricia Dabrowski, are very proud to continue the success, professionalism and traditions of the business founded so very long ago.

Top left: Centenary celebrations in 1956. **Above:** Part of the firm's fleet, a Mercedes limousine and hearse. **Left and inset:** Recent interior and exterior views of Ainsworth's Church Bank Street premises. **Below:** Directors Gregory and Patricia Dabrowski with daughter Melissa.

ACME Refrigeration
A Cool 50 Years!

The firm of ACME Refrigeration was established in August 1964. It began when two enterprising young businessmen, Mr James 'Jim' Hurley and Mr Hendrik Christiaan Caspar 'Peter' Hendriks, were touting their refrigeration wares around the same shops in the Blackburn area.

Jim Hurley is Blackburn born and bred and worked for his brother Clive in his refrigeration company until setting up on his own at the age of 21; he is still a director 50 years on. Peter Hendricks was born in Holland and settled in Blackburn in 1959 following service in the Dutch Navy. He then worked with an international refrigeration company.

The pair decided to pool their resources and join forces. Peter Hendriks looked after the operational side of the business whilst Jim Hurley was very much the salesman – it is said that he could sell snow to the eskimos

Originally, the business was predominantly selling refrigerated counters and deep freezers to local butchers, bakers and confectioners in the days before supermarkets, when there was a shop on every street corner.

ACME's first premises were in a small dairy in Hutton Street. Then, as and when more space was required, the business moved to other buildings in and around the town - an old church in Anvil Street, a school in Greenfield Street and another in Lambeth Street. In the summer of 1974 ACME's biggest move was to a brand new purpose-built factory and showroom on the Whitebirk Industrial Estate, Blackburn, where it settled for 34 years.

In 1984, when the company was 20 years old, it was acquired by Pentland Group PLC, which is a privately held global brand management British company. The Group is based in London and is a huge umbrella which ACME happily sits under.

Top left: *Founders, Peter Hendriks and Jim Hurley.*
Above: *Early premises in Lambeth Street school c1970.*
Below: *ACME's main building and fleet in the mid-1980s.*

Peter Hendricks moved to Spalding (Lincs) in 1985 following the sale of his share of the business. Sadly, he passed away in 2013 at the age of 78.

In 2008, the business moved just down the road to its current address – H&H House. Interestingly, the official name of the business, H&H Refrigeration is formed by the initials of the surnames of ACME's founders – Hurley and Hendricks, names recognised and respected to this very day.

ACME's products have certainly stood the test of time. Over the past half-century, the company has moved, not only with the times, but has been ahead of them in the unique and specialised world of refrigeration.

ACME has diversified into the catering equipment business to meet the needs of the many restaurateurs, licensees, confectioners and professional food suppliers around Blackburn and throughout the North of England.

ACME, both then and now, sources the latest and very best refrigeration equipment from all over the world, and the company has developed considerable respect from foreign manufacturers who now modify their equipment to meet the exacting specifications that ACME requires.

The company is an important employer within the local area, and currently two thirds of employees live within a 10 mile radius of H&H House.

At its outset the firm had only four employees, the two founders plus their wives, who helped with the administration. Today, the company has 110 staff.

Over the years, as the company has grown and expanded, many employees have been very loyal to the company and several key personnel have over 30 years service with ACME. They have played an important part in the business and have contributed to its success.

In commercial terms, ACME is defined as a medium sized company but in real terms, is a 'big hitter' within its industry. There is little the company cannot do – from design to installation – of the most specialised types of refrigeration - chiller rooms and cabinets, beer cellar cooling and air-conditioning. Among some unusual requests that have graced the order books this past half-century have been for large blocks of ice for use in ice sculptures, blood storage units for the Middle East, and ACME engineers frequently attend mortuaries throughout the North of England to service and maintain our penultimate places of rest!

Acme has enjoyed steady, year-on-year growth to today's multi-million pound turnover, and plans to develop this further to offer its established 24/7 coverage throughout the whole of the UK.

Top: ACME's H&H House, 2014. *Above:* One of ACME's current Transit vans. *Below:* A computer generated example of commercial kitchen design available from ACME.

The Mall
The Centre of Shopping

According to some accounts Blackburn has been a place to do one's shopping since 567 AD. Rather more certainly, in 1101 AD an earlier market was relocated in an area bounded by Church Street, Darwen Street, Mill Lane, Market Street Lane and Astley Gate. Robert de Lacy erected a Market Cross at the top of Church Street, but it was completely destroyed during the Civil War in 1642 and was never replaced.

Today, The Mall Blackburn, formerly named Blackburn Shopping Centre, is the shopping centre situated at the heart of the town. The Mall took ownership of the shopping centre in September 2004.

As with many other 'Mall' shopping centres in Britain, The Mall Blackburn has undergone major redevelopment and modernisation. TV screens 'Ask Me' points and other enhanced information is already provided and brand new areas such as a Primark and WH Smiths have been built. As well as the modernisation of the shopping centre, The Mall has introduced 'spend me' cards which are available at the centre.

The first phase of the shopping centre was built in 1964. Those who were around then will recall the times as one of immense hope and confidence in the future. Newly-elected Prime Minister Harold Wilson promised that the 'white heat of technology' would transform our lives. Modernism was the

watchword of the decade. And with an economy booming as never before that is what we got.

Phase two of the building work commenced in 1969 and in 1977 phase three. By 1996 however, it was looking tired and a refurbishment took place for most of the shopping centre with the exception of Lord Square.

The Mall acquired the shopping centre in September 2004. Year 2008 saw the start of a £66 million redevelopment programme. Demolition took place on Church Street and Lord Square including the old T J Hughes building. Vinci was appointed as the Design and Build contractor: during 2009 ground works, steel structure and internal building took place.

As work progressed the existing clock tower was demolished making way for a new 21st century clock tower, designed to enhance shopper safety and provide a focal point for consumers in the town's King William Street shopping hub.

The first phase of the redevelopment was completed on 26 July 2010 and consisted of an additional 200,000 sq. ft. of retail space and parking for 1,300 cars.

Pictures: *Images of Blackburn Shopping Centre prior to the 2008 redevelopments.*

Existing retailers Next, New Look and WH Smiths relocated to larger units in the new extension and a number of new retailers came to the town including Primark, Costa Coffee, H&M, Deichmann Shoes, Bank, USC and Pandora. The Mall was also refurbished and upgraded to include new Mall toilets and a management suite.

On 1st June 2011 the Council opened its 70,000 sq. ft. continental style Market consisting of over 100 stalls. It is located at street level and accessible from Church Street and Ainsworth Street.

In the early 1960s a proposal was made to move the Market to a new under cover site and to build a brand new shopping centre. The river Blakewater was culverted and the new Market opened in 1964. The local market still retained its traditional feel and was the second biggest in the country.

The market offered Lancashire specialities such as locally produced cheeses and black puddings. A trip to the market wasn't complete without a visit to Walsh's chemist stall where glasses of traditional sarsaparilla were served. The indoor market also boasted an excellent fish market.

Late in 2009 it was decided that the 1960s building was no longer fit for purpose and the market as we know it today, part of The Mall, was conceived.

Today, The Mall now comprises approximately 600,000 sq ft of retail space and dominates the retail offer in the town. It currently has 115 units, of which 100 are trading, including Debenhams, BHS, Boots, Primark, Next and Topshop as well as a number of independent retailers.

The Mall has successfully changed the face of retail in the town providing an improved retail offering which is attracting shoppers from across Lancashire and beyond – as Blackburn has enthusiastically been doing for a thousand years.

Pictures: Interior and exterior views of The Mall in 2014 showcasing why it is the first port of call for shopping in and around Blackburn.

Precision Polymer Engineering
Sealing Success

Seals are some of the most vital components within any piece of industrial equipment or system and without them the equipment does not work. Precision Polymer Engineering - PPE - is a sealing solutions provider, offering a combination of the correct elastomer (rubber) material and the most appropriate seal design, which ensures that equipment life is extended, mitigating costly downtime and repairs.

PPE was founded by Peter Cummings and remained a privately owned company until acquisition by the USA-based IDEX Corporation in 2010.

Some of PPE's earliest moulded rubber products were turntable mats for record players, loudspeaker surrounds and pressure cooker seals. These are considered very low-tech products by today's standards.

Originally, PPE moulded O-rings and custom-shaped components from standard elastomers. These materials were relatively low-tech, cheap and easily sourced, so for these commodity seals there were a number of competitors. Over the years, customers demanded seals capable of operating in more complex and arduous conditions, so PPE became a niche manufacturer specialising in hi-tech materials for the most difficult sealing applications. Today, PPE offers over 200 different grades of elastomer material to suit a broad range of sealing requirements.

The company was initially a 'one-man-band' with Peter Cummings doing everything including procurement, sales, moulding, packaging and delivery. As the business grew, a small team drove the business forward and some of these people are still employed at PPE today, which currently employs 270 people globally.

The firm started out based at Barn Meadow Lane, Great Harwood – a small run down building similar in size to a domestic garage. The business operated two small moulding presses, but when orders came in for larger components, a hole was made in the roof to crane a larger press into the premises.

In 1982, PPE moved to a unit in Waterfall Mill, Peel Street, Blackburn and then onto Clarendon Road, Skew Bridge, Blackburn, in 1987. The company moved to its present location, a purpose-built facility at Greenbank Road, Blackburn, in June 2003 and was officially opened by Rt. Hon. Jack Straw MP.

Top: PPE's purpose-built Greenbank Road, Blackburn, facility. *Left:* A turntable mat, one of the first products manufactured in the early 1970s. *Above right:* Where it all began, Barn Meadow Lane, Great Harwood. *Below:* PPE's Community League football team in 1997; three team members are still with PPE.

Outgrowing premises and lack of capacity on manufacturing equipment led PPE to continually invest in additional equipment, optimise/streamline its operating processes and expand its premises. An extension in 2009 at Greenbank Road almost doubled the size of the factory and added a new customer training facility.

As the business has grown, many new employees have joined the high number of long-service employees, some who have been with the company for more than 30 years.

Today, PPE's products are used worldwide in the oil and gas industry, chemical processing, food and pharmaceutical manufacturing, large diesel engines for marine propulsion and power generation, aerospace engines and semiconductor manufacturing.

PPE's customers include original equipment manufacturers and end users that require seals for critical applications. Often these applications have high costs or serious consequences associated with seal failure. Examples include pumps, valves, compressors, oil drilling tools, aircraft engines, Formula One racing cars, petrochemical plants, industrial food processing equipment, pharmaceutical manufacturing equipment, power

generating stations and silicon chip manufacturers. PPE also sells through a network of international dealers/distributors that have customers with specialist sealing requirements.

Operating at the forefront of elastomer technology, and continually looking to develop the next generation of sealing materials, PPE exports 80% of its output. This was recognised in 2007 with a Queen's Award for Enterprise in the International Trade category. The previous year (2006) PPE received a Queen's Award for Enterprise in the Innovation category for its work on inventing/developing brand new elastomer materials for the semiconductor industry.

Today, the company is looking forward to expanding its international reach by partnering with specialist sales distributors in countries around the world. Ambitious growth plans also include the acquisition of complimentary companies to create a group of companies that will form the Sealing Solutions division of IDEX Corporation.

Top left: PPE's former Clarendon Road, Skew Bridge, Blackburn, premises. *Left:* A selection of parts manufactured by PPE today. *Below left:* High performance O-rings typically used in critical equipment. *Above:* The Rt. Hon. Jack Straw MP tours the PPE factory at Greenbank Road in 2005. *Below:* High purity seals for semiconductor equipment manufactured in PPE's cleanroom.

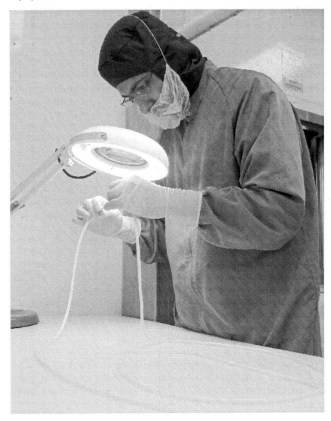

Parkinson Signs
Signs of Excellence

One of Blackburn's longest established family-owned businesses is Parkinson Signs Ltd, based in Chapel Street. It's a company which has done more than most to brighten Blackburn.

The firm was founded in 1946 by Arnold Parkinson. Having trained as an electrician, Arnold had earlier worked at the Star Paper Mill, then, during the war, at Mullard's.

Joined by an ex-Mullard's work colleague and friend, John Worden, the partnership which would become Parkinson & Worden Ltd first operated from the front room of No. 29 Brothers Street. In 1948 they moved to 49 King Street, next to the old Court House, where the business expanded to employ eight people, not least Alan Walmsley and William Lightbown who remained with the firm until their retirements in 1998 and 1997 respectively.

In the early days, the majority of business was making neon and cold cathode tube signs. Some of the big names such as Spiller Flour Mills and Walker's Steel were illuminated by Parkinson's lighting. Arnold Parkinson liked to reminisce how the famous local businessman Jack Walker of Walker's Steel (later to become one of Britain's richest men and benefactor of Blackburn Rovers), delivered steel to Parkinson & Worden by horse and hand cart in his early days.

In 1960, the business moved to 12/14 Chapel Street, a former Hindle Saw Mill, which is still the company base. Later

expansion included the purchase of cottages on Freckleton Street and Chapel Street.

In the early 1960s, one of Blackburn's most notable landmarks was created by Parkinson & Worden – ten-feet-high letters on the illuminated Thwaites' tower. This was a very prestigious contract of which the Company remains proud: the letters are still maintained by Parkinson's.

John Worden left the business in 1969, and Arnold's son, Gordon Parkinson, joined the firm from a background in electrical engineering. The business continued to expand and found a wide market in the brewing industry, specialising in signage on pubs for local brewers such as Whitbreads (formerly Thomas Duttons), Matthew Brown (formerly Nuttalls) and Thwaites.

*Top left: Founder, Arnold Parkinson. **Left:** Walkers & Sons signage by Parkinsons in the 1970s. **Above:** Gordon Parkinson. **Bottom left and below:** Thwaites tower's ten-feet-high lettering created by Parkinsons.*

The firm now started to specialise in other areas of signage, not least for the banking sector, obtaining national contracts with both Natwest and TSB.

Parkinson & Worden grew to employ up to 35 people, but still keeping its staff of many years service, such as Brian Fray and Albert Taylor, who retired with a combined total of 54 years' service.

Company founder Arnold Parkinson died in 1986. This left the firm solely in the hands of his son Gordon. Arnold's grandson Ian Parkinson subsequently joined the business direct from school at the age of 18 and proceeded to learn the business from the ground up – starting as a delivery driver and eventually working his way up to become Managing Director.

Down the decades the firm has consistently embraced the most modern technology, but, whilst updating machinery and processes, it has done so without sacrificing old fashioned quality and a close attention to customer service. In 2005, as part of a modernisation of the company image, the name of Parkinson & Worden Ltd was changed to the simpler, more direct Parkinson Signs Ltd.

Gordon Parkinson retired in 2007 leaving the firm in the hands of Ian Parkinson. Many of the firm's clientele are still in the same or related businesses as they were 40 years or more ago.

In 2009, Parkinson's provided a new image for Edmondson's Furniture, on Darwen Street, another long-standing family firm.

Most recently, investments have been made in new printing machinery, helping keep Parkinson's at the forefront of the industry.

Over the last four years, the firm has transformed Thwaites Brewery pubs with a new image making most of the produce in-house and revitalising the properties with a modern look.

Parkinson's also had a commission to make a Scotland Yard-style sign at Blackpool Football Club.

Recently the company has been asked to manufacture a series of 3D large fibreglass bees celebrating the three bees of Blackburn in the town's coat of arms. These are appearing all over the town with support from sponsors.

Parkinson Signs Ltd is proud of its heritage; it looks forward to not only sustaining, but enhancing, a reputation for excellence handed down from its founders to the present generation.

Top left: A sign created by Parkinsons for Dutton's. ***Above left:*** *Ian Parkinson, Managing Director, 2014.* ***Bottom left:*** *Signage for Thwaites' Black Bull.* ***Centre:*** *One of the 3D large fibreglass bees manufactured by Parkinsons.* ***Top right:*** *New Signage for Thwaites' Plough & Harrow.* ***Above:*** *The Scotland Yard style sign made for Blackpool F.C.* ***Below:*** *Parkinson Signs Chapel Street Works premises.*

Heritage Envelopes
Pushing the Envelope

Envelopes are something we all take for granted. Yet millions of them are used every day. Until the advent of the Penny Post, however, few envelopes were used. Before then letters were simply folded over and sealed with wax, the address being written on the outside.

Envelopes were at first manufactured individually by hand, a laborious and time-consuming operation.

The first patent for an efficient, automatic, envelope-making machine was registered in England in 1845.

Since then massive strides in envelope-making technology have been made. And few firms in the world have made better use of that technology than Blackburn's Heritage Envelopes Ltd, based on Davyfield Road. The company produces over two billion envelopes every year using some of the most advanced machines in the world.

Heritage Envelopes was founded in 1985 by John Jackson and David Sears. Their small enterprise was based in Horwich, Greater Manchester. In the first year turnover, using a single Smithe Rema envelope-making machine, was just over half a million pounds. With sales struggling, David Sears' father, Tom, was appointed Managing Director.

In the second year, turnover reached £1 million and the business became a limited company. In 1987, the firm moved to the team's home town of Darwen, where a second Smithe Rema machine was acquired and turnover rose to £1.2 million. The following year yet a third machine was bought.

In 1989, David's brother Mark joined the firm as an adjuster, and a fourth machine was installed in the growing factory. Tom Sears passed away in 1990 by which time annual turnover had reached £2.5 million.

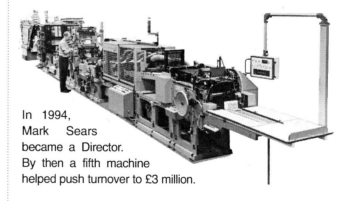

In 1994, Mark Sears became a Director. By then a fifth machine helped push turnover to £3 million.

The business moved to Lower Darwen in 1996 where a powerful second-hand Winkler & Dunnebier 102 machine was installed. The following year three more used W&D 102s were bought, and turnover reached £6 million.

Top: Heritage Envelopes' Heritage House, Davyfield Road, premises. *Centre left:* The company's first machine, a Smithe Rema M/c. *Left:* Tom Sears, Managing Director from 1986 to 1990. *Above:* Heritage Envelopes' first WD 102, acquired in 1999.

Yet another three pre-owned W&D 102 machines were acquired in 1998 and the original Smithe Rema machines taken out of production.

Ian Walmsley joined the company as Sales Manager in 1999, John Jackson became Operations Director and Mark Sears Sales & Technical Director.

A move was now made to a new 100,000 sq. ft. purpose-built premises in Blackburn, where turnover was soon pushed to over £8 million. That year the first brand-new W&D 102 machine was installed. Two more were acquired in 2000, as were two 'Diamond' over-printing machines.

In 2001, turnover reached £14.5 million. The company exchanged its Diamond over-printers for machines from Winkler & Dunnebier – and two old W&D 102s were replaced by new ones, as were two more 102s in 2002.

A four colour over-printer was acquired in 2002. By now Ian Walmsley was Sales Director and Martyn Salt Logistics Director. In 2004, with turnover of £19 million, Heritage made its biggest commercial decision going into partnership with GPV Groupe.

In 2007, with the takeover of full control by GPV, a new management structure was put in place with Mark Sears heading the organisation as Managing Director of Heritage and of sister company Chapman Envelopes Ltd. In 2011, the GPV Groupe attracted the attention of the Mayer-Kuvert-Network GmbH, which now acquired GPV. With Mark Sears as CEO Heritage now formed part of the largest envelope group in Europe.

In 2012, the Mayer network consolidated its UK operations by closing Eagle and Chapman Envelopes and moving production to Heritage. Being part of the Mayer group has allowed investment in areas other than machinery, including maintenance, apprenticeship schemes and management training courses. This ensures that Heritage Envelopes remains the leading envelope manufacturer in the UK. Heritage Envelopes is constantly evolving and working towards the future, providing banks, financial institutions and other blue chip organisations with a reliable source of envelopes. At any one time there is over 1,000 tonnes of various paper in stock at the Blackburn site. Production is in excess of 50 million envelopes per week powered by 15 W&D envelope

machines. The production system is designed to ensure that the company can offer shorter lead-times than its competitors and provide unrivalled effectiveness and efficiency in the services it provides to its customers.

Today, annual turnover is in excess of £24 million and growing. Envelopes are clearly something one can't take for granted.

*Above: Mark Sears, CEO. **Top left and below:** Views Inside Heritage Envelopes' 100, 000 sq. ft. purpose-built factory.*

Robinsons Holidays
Journey Through Time with Robinsons Holidays From 1923 to Today!

It is hard to believe looking at the fleet of modern comfort class coaches at Robinsons Holidays of Great Harwood that it all started in the very same yard in 1923 by the Robinson family. Originally farmers, the family started up and operated their own coach company from their existing farm land and utilized their barn as their first garage. The same land today (Park Garage at Great Harwood) is still used by the company.

Today's Robinsons Holidays passengers travelling in these luxury coaches can either be picked up from one of over 160 departure points or take the option of door-to-door transport from their own homes and they don't need to handle their luggage as there is an 'integrated luggage handling service' unlike those passengers of 1923 who would have had a far less luxurious ride than their counterparts today, no 'comfort classes for them, or reclining seats, air conditioning or toilet facilities! Instead, they would be seated in the back of open lorries with solid tires and fixed bench wooden seats for their day trips to the seaside.

In 1948, ownership of Robinsons transferred to the family-owned Holdsworth Group and it still remains part of the Holdsworth Group today. The company expanded in 1982 with the purchase of another local coach company, Ribblesdale Coachways. One of their main contracts was providing transport for the pupils of Westholme School, which Robinsons continue to do to this day.

Robinsons have over the years been extremely fortunate in having a loyal and faithful following with passengers remaining loyal to the company, possibly because of its

Top left: Frank Kemp stands proudly in front of his 1950s Bedford SB coach. *Above:* A picture of how the original Bedford SB of the 1950s with a butterfly front, would have looked in its green and black Robinsons livery. *Below:* A Robinsons coach of the 1950s - it has a Moseley engine with a Plaxton body.

family origins, ethos and name which have remained. Most passengers travel by feeder coach to the interchange point at Lymm in Cheshire or other central points, from as far north as Barrow and as far south as Birmingham. An increasing number of passengers are making use of the door-to-door service, which picks up at home and goes directly to the main tour coach.

Passengers frequently return year after year and many have several holidays each year, finding comfortable surroundings and companionship.

Robinsons continue to update the coach fleet, and build on the popular holiday destinations, seasonal and festive breaks and private hire availability to suit the needs of existing and new passengers

As well as enjoying a loyal passenger following, Robinsons also have been fortunate in having a loyal and committed workforce with many employees remaining with the company for all of their working careers. Many of Robinsons staff have over the years provided photos and memories of tours of former decades to add to the company's historical archives, some of

which are shown in this article. One of Robinsons dedicated engineers is also a passionate collector of old Robinsons coaches which he adds to his own private collection of vehicles.

Top: Group photographs like this were typical of tours of the 1950s and 60s- this one shows the party, the driver (Frank Kemp - front row far right - seated), and the coach - a 1950s Bedford SB. *Left:* A typical Robinsons coach of the 1980s - a Leyland Tigers in their then familiar green and black livery. *Above:* Retired but not too old for restoring to its former glory! - the 1956 Bedford SB XTB 91 on its way home again to Robinsons. It was tracked down by Robinsons employee William Brayford, an enthusiast and collector. *Below:* The latest addition to Robinsons' fleet of luxury coaches.

Acknowlegements

The publishers would like to sincerely thank the following individuals and organisations for their help and contribution to this publication.

Mary Painter - Blackburn with Darwen Library & Information Service

Mirrorpix

Ben Brooksbank